THE LIFE OF GRACE

THE LIFE OF GRACE

Faith and Life Series

Revised Edition

BOOK SEVEN

Ignatius Press, San Francisco
Catholics United for the Faith, Steubenville, Ohio

Nihil Obstat: Rev. James M. Dunfee, S.T.L.
                Censor Librorum
Imprimatur: + Most Reverend Bishop R. Daniel Conlon
                Bishop of Steubenville

Director of First Edition: The late Rev. Msgr. Eugene Kevane, Ph.D.
Assistant Director and General Editor of First Edition: Patricia Puccetti Donahoe, M.A.
First Edition Writer: David R. Previtali
Director and General Editor of Revision: Caroline Avakoff, M.A.
Revision Writer: Colette Ellis, M.A.
Revision Artist: Christopher J. Pelicano

Catholics United for the Faith, Inc., and Ignatius Press gratefully acknowledge the guidance and assistance of the late Reverend Monsignor Eugene Kevane, Director of the Pontifical Catechetical Institute, Diocese of Arlington, Virginia, in the production of the First Edition of this series. The First Edition intended to implement the authentic approach in Catholic catechesis given to the Church through documents of the Holy See and in particular the Conference of Joseph Cardinal Ratzinger on "Sources and Transmission of Faith." The Revised Edition continues this commitment by drawing upon the *Catechism of the Catholic Church* (Libreria Editrice Vaticana, © 1994).

Scripture quotations are from the Holy Bible, Revised Standard Version, Catholic Edition. Old Testament © 1952; Apocrypha © 1957; Catholic Edition, incorporating the Apocrypha, © 1966; New Testament © 1946; Catholic Edition © 1965, by the Division of Christian Education of the National Council of the Churches of Christ in the United States of America. All rights reserved.

The Ad Hoc Committee to Oversee the Use of the Catechism, United States Conference of Catholic Bishops, has found this catechetical text to be in conformity with the *Catechism of the Catholic Church.*

Contents

APPENDIX

A Note to Parents about the Revision

The changes to the seventh grade student text, *The Life of Grace*, while minimal, attempt to emphasize the scriptural basis of our Faith in accord with Sacred Tradition. New vocabulary is now indicated by bold type, new words have been introduced to enhance each lesson in the revised text, and each definition can now be found both within the chapter and in the glossary. Common Catholic prayers have been included in an expansive list at the back of the student textbook. In addition, every chapter opens with a Scripture passage, important verses supplement the text where relevant, new questions have been introduced, pre-existing questions have been revised for age-appropriateness, and references to the *Catechism of the Catholic Church* are now specified for each question and answer.

Despite the improvements to the series, it is important to realize that, as parents, you are the primary educators of your children. Your active participation in your child's religious education is highly encouraged. As a family, you are the first witnesses of God's love to your child. If you provide a model of Catholic living at home, if as a family you participate in the sacramental life of the Church, and if you pray and attend Mass together, your children are more likely to take to heart the lessons they learn in religion classes at school. Family discussion of current events with a healthy religious perspective will allow your child to grow up with a better understanding of the world around him, and more importantly, help him to be a Catholic in the midst of it. As stated in the General Directory for Catechesis, "family catechesis precedes . . . accompanies and enriches all forms of catechesis" (GDC, 226; Congregation for the Clergy, 1998). Providing your child with a strong Catholic identity at an early age, while not ensuring a lifetime of devotion, will certainly prepare him for the challenges of becoming a faithful Catholic adult.

The Life of Grace student text is written on a reading level higher than that of the average seventh grader. This is intentional. It is important for children to hear the Good News in a fuller manner than a more simplified version would allow. Please take the time to review the material with your children, to read the text aloud with them, to study the questions and answers, and to examine and discuss the religious art that accompanies each chapter. By lessening the emphasis on individual student reading, there is more opportunity for your child to concentrate on the Gospel message itself as well as the idea that theology plays an important role in all aspects of his life.

Those who have labored in the revision process of the Faith and Life series sincerely hope that it will provide parents, catechists, and teachers with the assistance they need in the task of evangelizing young minds.

INTRODUCTION

From the beginning of man's creation God has communicated with the human race in order to share with us his life and his love. He has told us about himself and has shown us how we are to live if we hope to reach heaven, our eternal home.

Through the wonders of nature he gives us a reflection of his power and his glory. In the events and lives of the people of the Old Testament he reveals himself as Lord and leader of his chosen people. In the New Testament and teachings of the Catholic Church, God gives us his greatest revelation: Jesus Christ, the Son of God become man.

In Jesus we see the perfect image of God: loving, merciful, forgiving, and eager to share with us his own divine life. This life, called sanctifying grace, is communicated to each one of us through the seven sacraments of the Church. Each of these sacraments helps us as we travel toward heaven; in each of them we meet Jesus, who gives us strength for our pilgrimage.

Through the sacraments Christ unites us with himself, deepening the life of God within us and helping us to become better Christians. Through these sacred ceremonies Jesus is with us all through our lives. At Baptism he first comes to us and makes us children of the Father. Confirmation strengthens this new life in our souls and helps us to remain faithful to Our Lord and his Church. Holy Eucharist nourishes our souls. Penance heals us and gives the life of God back to our souls if we lose it by mortal sin. Holy Orders and Matrimony help Christians to serve God and the Church. Anointing of the Sick strengthens us when we are seriously ill and prepares us for a holy death.

In our study of the faith we will see how the sacraments are very important for our lives in Christ and the Church. By receiving them properly, with faith, hope, and love, we will become more and more worthy of entering the everlasting joys of heaven, our true home.

PART ONE

God Reveals Himself

CHAPTER 1

Knowing God Through Creation

Let the earth bless the Lord; let it sing praise to him and highly exalt him for ever.

Daniel 3:52

No person should ever be ignorant of God's existence. By using the reasoning powers of our minds we can come to know that there is a God, who created the wonderful world in which we live. This is true even for those who do not have the **gift of faith**. The great apostle Saint Paul reminded the Christians of Rome about this truth:

Ever since the creation of the world his [God's] invisible nature, namely, his eternal power and deity, has been clearly perceived in the things that have been made (Rom 1:20).

Everywhere in the universe we find *order* and *design*. Order and design are sure signs of God's hand in creation. To explain order and design as the results of "chance" is really quite foolish. For example, consider an ordinary wrist watch. Do you believe that it just happened to come into existence? Is it possible that the metal out of which it is made happened to form itself into the shape of a watch? Even more astonishing, could the numbers on its face "just happen" to arrange themselves in the proper order and with just the right amount

of space so as to keep perfect time? Of course not! Then consider the many wondrous things in the universe, a billion times more complex than a watch: the solar system, an insect, the individuality of each human body. Do you think that these things just happened without anyone commanding and directing their creation?

Along with knowing that God exists, we are able to learn a little about him through the study of creation. By seeing the great power of the ocean with its waves and tides, we learn that its Maker must be great and powerful as well. The beautiful aromas and colors of spring flowers tell us that their Creator must be pleasing and beautiful too. All of God's creatures tell us something about him; they all reflect a bit of his greatness, beauty, and power.

Learning about Ourselves through Reason

Just as we can come to know about God by the use of our reasoning power, so we are able to learn about ourselves by examining our own selves, our desires, and our actions. One of the first things we notice is that we have a body

much like some animals. We have legs in order to walk and eyes with which to see. This reminds us that we are a part of God's *physical creation.*

When we consider the differences between the animals and us, however, we see that human beings are different from the animals in two important ways. Human beings are intelligent and free. With our minds we understand things, and with our free will we control our actions in ways that animals cannot. Our powers to understand and to choose show that we have a spiritual part that animals lack. This part is man's spiritual soul. Thus, human beings have physical bodies, like the animals, but they also have spiritual souls, which animals do not have.

Our spiritual nature makes us like God himself. This is why the Bible says that human beings were made "in the image of God" (Gen 1:27). Like God, we can know and understand. Like God, we can freely choose. Like God, we are persons.

God created many different kinds of creatures and made them dependent on one another in many ways. He intended man to use his reason and freedom to care for the material world around him. God also gave the material creation to man for the good of the human race. The minerals, plants, and animals of our world God gave us to appreciate and use properly. That includes making sure everyone has his rightful share of what he needs to live and that everyone respects what belongs to others.

Human Reason and the Gift of Faith

As wonderful as the human mind is, it can tell us only so much when it comes to God and the purpose of human life. We need God's help when it comes to the great mysteries of our faith. We need God himself to reveal things to us. **Revelation** is the word we use for the things that God has told us about himself and about his purpose for us. Another name for God's revelation is the word of God.

Revelation is a gift from God. In order for us to accept it as true, God gives us another gift, the **gift of faith**. Faith makes it possible for us to believe what God has revealed. By faith, we freely and firmly say "yes" to what God has told us. When we refer to "the Faith," we mean the **Catholic Faith**, the body of truths that we believe as Catholics. We can say "yes" to those truths because God has revealed them, and he has given us the gift of faith to believe them.

Revelation Perfects Our Knowledge of God

As we have seen, **human reason** can tell us certain things about God—for example, that he exists. At the same time, God has revealed certain things about himself and he gives us faith to enable us to believe what he has revealed. Yet even when we believe, we do not stop using our minds. Reason can help us understand what we believe and why we believe that God has revealed it, even if reason cannot completely understand everything that God has revealed. Sometimes reason can even show us that we should believe—that it is the reasonable thing to do. For instance, when we look at the great miracles of Jesus, reason tells us that we should believe what Jesus said. Only someone sent from God could do the things Jesus did—turning water into wine, healing blind people, and rising from the dead.

We have talked about things we can know about God from reason and things we can know about God only through revelation. But the things we can know about God by reason he has also chosen to reveal. Why? He did this to make sure that even if someone does not come to know such truths on his own, he can still come to them through revelation and faith. Thus, we can see that faith and reason go together and can help each other.

The Bible teaches us many things about God. For example, it tells us that he is everywhere. As a pure spirit, he is not limited by a physical body to any one time and place. The Psalmist asks God:

Whither shall I go from thy Spirit? Or whither shall I flee from thy presence? If I ascend to heaven, thou art there! If I make my bed in Sheol, thou art there! If I take the wings of the morning and dwell in the uttermost parts of the sea, even there thy hand shall lead me, and thy right hand shall hold me (Ps 139:7–10).

The Bible also says that God knows everyone and everything. He knows all that ever was, all that is, and all that ever will be:

He searches out the abyss, and the hearts of men, and considers their crafty devices. For the Most High knows all that may be known, and he looks into the signs of the age. He declares what has been and what is to be, and he reveals the tracks of hidden things. No thought escapes him, and not one word is hidden from him (Sir 42:18–20).

Some of what the Bible tells us about God we can also know by human reason. Other things we can know only through revelation and faith.

Jesus revealed the greatest truth about God: that there are three Persons in the one God. We call this the mystery of the **Trinity**. Jesus revealed the inner life of the one God, something no human being could come to know unless God revealed it, and it is something we must believe by faith. In the Trinity, there is God the Father (the First Person of the Holy Trinity), God the Son (the Second Person of the Holy Trinity, who became man as Jesus Christ), and God the Holy Spirit (the Third Person of the Holy Trinity). Each Person is distinct and not the others, yet each is God. The Trinity is a great **mystery** of faith—something beyond reason but not contrary to it.

Scripture also teaches that God is love (1 Jn 4:8). As an expression of his love, God chose to create our universe from nothing, and he made man only a little less than the angels, giving us the wonderful gift of reason. Out of this same love God revealed himself to us and gave us the gift of faith so that we can know him more deeply and believe what he has told us.

Words to Know:
revelation   gift of faith   mystery
Catholic Faith   human reason   Trinity

Q. 1   *Using reason can man know with certainty that there is a God?*
Yes, using reason man can know with certainty that there is a God, on the basis of his works (CCC 50).

Q. 2   *Can man understand God's plan through reason alone?*
No, man cannot understand God's plan through reason alone. Man must also rely upon faith and God's revelation (CCC 50).

Q. 3   *How has man come to know God as the Holy Trinity?*
Man has come to know God as the Holy Trinity through the revelation of Jesus Christ, the Son of God made man (CCC 240, 243).

Q. 4   *What is the Holy Trinity?*
The Holy Trinity is the mystery of the one true God in three
Divine Persons, Father, Son, and Holy Spirit (CCC 234).

Q. 5   *Who is the First Person of the Holy Trinity?*
God the Father is the First Person of the Holy Trinity (CCC
198, 238).

Q. 6   *Who is the Second Person of the Holy Trinity?*
God the Son is the Second Person of the Holy Trinity. The Son
became man in the Divine Person of Jesus Christ (CCC 240,
423).

Q. 7   *Who is the Third Person of the Holy Trinity?*
God the Holy Spirit is the Third Person of the Holy Trinity
(CCC 245, 685).

Q. 8   *Are the three Divine Persons of the Holy Trinity all
God?*
Yes, the three Divine Persons of the Holy Trinity are all God.
They share the same nature and substance (what something is),
and they are one God (CCC 253–55).

Q. 9   *Is any one Person of the Holy Trinity greater than the
others?*
No, the Persons of the Holy Trinity are all infinitely great. They
are all eternal. No one Person of the Holy Trinity is greater than
the others (CCC 202, 256).

Q. 10   *What is faith?*
Faith is the gift of God whereby man assents to and believes in
God and the truths he has revealed (CCC 153, 155).

CHAPTER 2

Divine Revelation

For you, brethren, became imitators of the churches of God in Christ Jesus which are in Judea; for you suffered the same things from your own countrymen as they did from the Jews, who killed both the Lord Jesus and the prophets, and drove us out, and displease God and oppose all men.

1 Thessalonians 2:14–15

In the first chapter we learned that by using our reasoning powers we are able to know that God exists. We also saw that human reason alone cannot discover all that there is to know about our Creator. Out of his great love, God has revealed himself to us first through the Jewish people of the Old Testament, and later in the life of Jesus, which is handed on to us in the teachings of the Church. We call the truths that God has made known to us **divine revelation.**

History of Divine Revelation

God did not simply reveal himself to one person at one point of time; he made himself known bit by bit. The first people to know him were Adam and Eve. Later God formed a chosen people, called the Israelites, who later became the Jews, to be the special keepers of his revelation.

He began forming this community by choosing a man named Abraham, who lived almost four thousand years ago in the land of Mesopotamia. God made him the father, or founder, of the chosen people. These people eventually wrote down the revelation they had received

from God. They collected these writings into a book that we call the **Old Testament**.

Almost two thousand years after Abraham the time came for God to give us his greatest revelation, the gift of his only Son, Jesus Christ. Our Lord taught the people all about God and corrected some wrong ideas they had about him. In order to make sure that his teachings would be correctly understood and passed on to others, he founded the Church. Jesus made his twelve apostles the official teachers in the Church and placed his revelation (gospel) in their safekeeping. After the Resurrection, the apostles taught the gospel to others both by preaching and by writing (the New Testament). Some Christians today do not believe that Tradition and Scripture are both necessary for true believers to learn the whole truth about God. But the Second Vatican Council reminded us that

Tradition and the Bible . . . join together and aim at the same goal. The Bible is the message of God put in writing under the inspiration of the Holy Spirit. Tradition delivers the word of God which

18

was entrusted by Christ and the Holy Spirit to the apostles and their successors. . . . So both Tradition and the Bible are to be accepted in the same way (*Dei verbum*, no. 9).

Sacred Scripture, the Bible, and Sacred **Tradition**, the Word of God given by Jesus to the Apostles and through them to their successors, contain the whole truth of God. It is very important to remember that divine revelation reached its greatest point with the life of Christ and the preaching of his twelve apostles. The Lord's teachings, faithfully preached by these holy men, are summed up in a profession of faith that we call the Apostles' Creed. Saint Augustine taught that the **Creed** is the summary of our faith and the key to correctly interpreting Sacred Scripture. This Creed is a statement of our basic beliefs as Catholic Christians; in it are found the main mysteries of our faith. A *mystery* is a truth that is above our power to understand fully, but which we believe because God has said that it is so.

When the last surviving apostle died (Saint John, ca. 100) God's public revelation of himself to the world *came to an end*. All that God wanted man to know for salvation had been made known by Jesus and his twelve apostles. As Vatican II stated, "There is to be no further public revelation until Christ comes again" (*Dei verbum*, no. 4).

The Holy Bible

The **Holy Bible**, also called Sacred Scripture, is the *inspired* Word of God; it is one of his greatest gifts to us. We usually think of the Bible as one book, but it is really a collection of seventy-three books, written by various men in different centuries. It is divided into two sections: the Old Testament and the New Testament.

The Old Testament

The first section of the Bible, the Old Testament, was put together by the Jewish people. It consists of the first forty-six books of the Bible which are chiefly concerned with preparing the world for the Messiah. There are three basic categories of Old Testament writings:

THE HISTORICAL BOOKS: the religious and historical traditions of the Jews. These books include the *Pentateuch* (the first five books of the Bible, called the "Torah" or Law of Moses by the Jews).

THE WISDOM BOOKS: a collection of prayers, wise sayings, and advice, often written in poetic forms.

THE PROPHETIC BOOKS: the words and messages of God's chosen spokesmen, the prophets. This category also includes the books of Lamentations and Baruch.

The New Testament

The second section of the Bible, the **New Testament**, is the most important part of the Scriptures, because it contains the life and teachings of Jesus. It too has different kinds of writings:

THE GOSPELS: The **Gospels** are the four accounts of Christ's life and message of salvation, written by the apostles Matthew and John, and the disciples Mark and Luke. They faithfully hand on to us what Jesus said and did when he lived on earth.

THE ACTS OF THE APOSTLES: This is a brief history of the early Church, primarily covering the ministry of Saint Peter and the missionary work of Saint Paul.

THE LETTERS OF SAINT PAUL: These are the teachings of Christ applied to particular needs of the early Church and to the daily life of the Christians.

THE LETTERS TO ALL CHRISTIANS: These were written by various apostles as catholic, or universal, teachings to all the believers.

THE BOOK OF REVELATION: Also called the Apocalypse, this book was written by the apostle John shortly before his death. It was meant to be a source of encouragement to the persecuted Church, reminding the believers that Jesus is victorious over all his enemies.

The Old and New Testaments are united in God's plan of revelation. The Old Testament prepares us for the New, and the New is understood in light of the Old. "The New Testament lies hidden in the Old and the Old Testament is unveiled in the New" (CCC 129).

Authorship and Inspiration of the Bible

We call the Scriptures the *Word of God* because their primary author was God the Holy Spirit. He chose certain men to be the *human* authors; they put down, in their own language and style, only what the Spirit *inspired* them to write. **Inspiration** means that God moved these men to write about him and he guided their minds as to what to put down.

Because God inspired men to write these books, they are free from all error in teaching us about God and what is necessary for our salvation. This freedom from error is called "inerrancy." It is important to remember that the Bible is meant to teach us religious truths, not necessarily the laws of science. For example, the ancient writers thought that the earth was at the center of the universe and that the sun and stars revolved around the earth. This mistaken view of science, however, has no effect on the truths which they wrote down about

God and our responsibilities toward him and to each other.

The Protector and Teacher Of Divine Revelation

Since God has given us his revelation through various people and in various forms, it makes sense that he would appoint someone to be the one true protector and teacher of these truths. After all, we are not dealing here with ordinary facts of life, but with the supernatural truths by which people are saved!

We saw earlier in this chapter that Jesus established his Church for this very purpose. He placed the Church in the hands of the apostles and their successors, saying:

All authority in heaven and on earth has been given to me. Go therefore and make disciples of all nations, baptizing them in the name of the Father and of the Son and of the Holy Spirit, teaching them to observe all that I have commanded you; and lo, I am with you always, to the close of the age (Mt 28:18–20).

The successors of the apostles today are the Pope (who takes Saint Peter's place of authority) and the Catholic bishops of the world. Their teaching authority is called the **Magisterium** or official teaching office of the church. It belongs to them alone (or to the Pope himself) to judge what is true Christian belief. The Magisterium guides the members of the Church of Our Lord in what must be believed and done by his faithful followers. Like the Twelve, the Pope and the bishops in union with him are guided by the Holy Spirit, who protects them from teaching any error in matters of faith and morals. This special gift is called **infallibility**. With Jesus' authority and power, the Pope and the bishops in union with him proclaim his good news of salvation. They show us how to live good Christian lives as we journey to heaven, our eternal home.

Words to Know:

New Testament   Old Testament
Tradition   Gospels   Holy Bible
inspiration   Creed   divine revelation
infallibility   Magisterium

Q. 11   *What is revelation?*
Revelation is God's communication to man in words and deeds, and most fully in the Person of Jesus Christ. Revelation is found in Sacred Scripture and Sacred Tradition (CCC 53, 65).

Q. 12   *What is Sacred Scripture?*
Sacred Scripture, also called the Bible, is the Word of God written by human authors under the inspiration of the Holy Spirit (CCC 81).

Q. 13 *What is Sacred Tradition?*

Sacred Tradition is the entire Word of God entrusted by Jesus Christ to the apostles, who in turn passed it on to their successors (CCC 81).

Q. 14 *Who safeguards and interprets revelation?*

The Magisterium, or the Teaching Church, safeguards and interprets revelation. The Pope and the bishops in union with him make up the Magisterium (CCC 85, 95).

Q. 15 *When did God's public revelation of himself end?*

God's public revelation of himself ended with the New Covenant offered in Jesus Christ. There will be no further public revelation before the Second Coming of our Lord (CCC 66).

Q. 16 *How is God the author of Sacred Scripture?*

God, as the author of Sacred Scripture, inspired the writers by the work of the Holy Spirit to write all that he wanted written and no more (CCC 105–06).

Q. 17 *What is the Old Testament?*

The Old Testament is the collection of sacred books intended to prepare God's people for the coming of Jesus Christ (CCC 122).

Q. 18 *What is the New Testament?*

The New Testament is the collection of sacred books that records the life and teachings of Jesus Christ, the Church's beginnings, and the teachings of the apostles (CCC 124, 126, 129).

Q. 19 *Is Sacred Scripture free from error?*

Yes, Sacred Scripture is free from error in that truth which God, for the sake of our salvation, wished to see recorded (CCC 107).

Q. 20   *What is infallibility?*
Infallibility, a gift of the Holy Spirit, protects the Church from teaching errors in matters of faith and morals (CCC 890–91).

Q. 21   *What is the Apostles' Creed?*
The Apostles' Creed is the summary and profession of faith in the chief mysteries and other truths revealed by God through Jesus Christ (CCC 187, 194).

Q. 22   *What is a mystery?*
A mystery is a truth beyond our reason, which is revealed by God (CCC 237).

Q. 23   *What are the chief mysteries of faith that we profess in the Creed?*
The chief mysteries of faith that we profess in the Creed are the Holy Trinity and the Incarnation, Passion, death, and Resurrection of Jesus Christ (CCC 189–90).

CHAPTER 3

Creation

In the beginning God created the heavens and the earth.

Genesis 1:1

God shares with us his beauty, his power, and his glory in the wonderful world which he created. The Holy Bible begins with the book of Genesis, in which we find the story of the world's creation. In order better to appreciate the almighty power of God we must know that to **create** means to make something out of *nothing*. The entire universe came into existence simply because God wanted it to exist! He did not use any materials to create the world as we must when we make something. Rather he had only to think of the universe and it was created! This is why the book of Genesis tells us that God had only to say, "Let there be light," and there was light (Gen 1:3).

The inspired story of creation was originally part of the oral tradition (religious stories) of the Jewish people. They passed this story on to each generation in order to teach and remind the people that:

1. *There is only one God and he is the Creator of all that exists*—the pagans often believed that each of their gods created different things in the world.

2. *God created the world in an orderly way and as a way of sharing his love with man*—many pagans believed that the world was the result of a war between their gods or that it happened by accident.

3. *Everything created by God is good*—the pagans believed many created things to be the work of an evil god who liked to make mankind suffer.

The Creation of Mankind

The book of Genesis also tells us about the creation of the first man and the first woman, the parents of the entire human race:

Then God said, "Let us make man in our image, after our likeness. . . ." So God created man in his own image, in the image of God he created him; male and female he created them. And God blessed them, and God said to them, "Be fruitful and multiply, and fill the earth and subdue it; and have dominion over the fish of the sea and over the birds of the air and over every living thing that moves upon the earth." And God said, "Behold, I have given you every plant yielding seed which is upon the face of all the earth, and every tree with seed in its fruit; you shall have them for food" (Gen 1:26–29).

This account tells us that God had a greater plan for man than he had for the rest of the world of nature; he gave man authority over the beasts and plants of the earth, which were created for man's proper use (such as food, clothing, or enjoyment of nature). The second chapter of Genesis gives us another account of creation.

> Then the LORD God said, "It is not good that the man should be alone; I will make him a helper fit for him." . . . So the LORD God caused a deep sleep to fall upon the man, and while he slept took one of his ribs and closed up its place with flesh; and the rib which the LORD God had taken from the man he made into a woman and brought her to the man (Gen 2:18–22).

The parents of the human race were called Adam and Eve, because Adam means "man," and Eve means "mother of the living."

The Human Person

In Genesis we see that after God made the human body, he "breathed into his nostrils the breath of life; and man became a living being" (Gen 2:7). This tells us that we are each composed of both a physical **body** and a spiritual **soul**. The body is made of matter (as are all things that can be touched, seen, etc.) and so this makes us like the beasts and other physi-

cal creatures. But the soul is *spiritual*; that is, like God it is invisible but real. This is why Scripture tells us that we are made in God's image and likeness; for we share with him in the world of the spirit and, unlike the other physical creatures, we will live *forever* since we have souls that are **immortal**.

The soul has two spiritual powers that make us very much like our Creator: the intellect and the will. By the power of the intellect we are able to think, reason, and know right from wrong. The will allows us to choose freely what we shall do or say or think; it gives us the ability to love or to hate, to do good or to sin. We all know that no other earthly creature can do these things.

Both the body and the soul are important to man, otherwise God would not have created them. Even though the soul is immortal and has great powers, without the body we would not be true and complete human beings. God commands that we respect and take care of both of these gifts which he has given us. God made all human beings persons. In that sense, "all men are created equal." That does not mean that everyone is exactly the same or that everyone is equally good, intelligent, or strong. It means that human beings all have the same basic dignity and rights from God. It also means that we should respect the rights of others, as we expect others to respect our rights.

God Gave Man Special Gifts

When God created Adam and Eve he gave them more than their natural bodies and souls; he gave them special gifts. These gifts were not part of man's nature, but enabled him to do things beyond his ordinary abilities. They had complete harmony and peace in their lives; they never argued or acted selfishly toward each other. Also, God kept them free from suffering, sickness, and death. But most of all he gave them a share in his own divine life with the gift of **sanctifying grace**. This grace made them more than his creatures: it made them his children and heirs to heaven, where they would live with him forever! These gifts would be theirs and would be passed on to all of their descendants. In this way, human beings were destined to share in God's glory, and, through man, the whole material creation would share God's glory. All that was required of the man and the woman was that they love and serve him all their lives.

The Creation of the Angels

Before we look at the events that led to man's loss of these gifts, we must know that God first created, from nothing, pure spirits whom we call angels. They are intelligent persons like us but they do not have physical bodies as we do, they are spiritual beings without bodies. Angels possess greater intelligence and power than human beings, but they too were created to worship and serve God.

God put the angels to a test to give them a chance to love him freely and obey his commands. Some of them, led by Lucifer, refused to serve the Lord; they rebelled against him. So God created **hell**, where those who do not want to be with him are sent. These angels were good when they were created by God, but they became evil by their own free choice. We call these disobedient spirits **fallen angels** or *demons*. They are still led by Lucifer, who is also known as satan or the devil. They try to turn all creation away from God, for they do not want God's creatures to serve him.

The spirits who loved God and obeyed his commands are called *faithful* or **good angels**; they were led by Michael the Archangel. These angels assist us in living holy Christian lives so that we will serve God on earth and come to live with him in heaven when we die. God has assigned a good angel to each one of us; this angel is called our *guardian angel* and his mission is to help us on our way to heaven.

The Fall of Man

Like the angels, God tested our first parents to give them the choice to love and serve him freely. He gave Adam and Eve a beautiful garden in which to live, the Garden of Eden (also called Paradise), and he told them that they could eat anything in that garden except the fruit of the tree of the knowledge of good and evil.

The devil saw this as an opportunity to lead Adam and Eve away from God. He entered the garden and tempted our first parents to sin. He said that if they ate the fruit of the forbidden tree they would become just like their Creator!

Poor Adam and Eve! They believed the lies of satan and ate the forbidden fruit. At that moment they knew that they had sinned, and they were filled with shame. They tried to hide from God, which is, of course, an impossible thing to do.

The Lord called to them and told Adam and Eve that they must now be banished from the Garden of Eden and be subject to suffering, sickness, and death. Much worse, they would no longer live in the state of sanctifying grace which had made them the children and friends of God, heirs to the happiness of **heaven**. Now they could not pass on God's special gifts. In fact, now they passed on to their descendants a human nature that was weakened because of their sin.

We call this sin of Adam **original sin** because it was the first sin ever to be committed by man and because it is passed on from Adam, the origin of the human race. The terrible results of this sin (separation from God, sickness, death, slavery to sin and the devil) are called the *effects* of original sin. Except for Jesus and Mary, all human beings since the time of Adam and Eve have been conceived with original sin and its effects on their souls.

We must not think that God was unfair in taking away these gifts; they were gifts freely given and not deserved. In his love he clearly told Adam and Eve what the result of their disobedience would be when he said:

You may freely eat of every tree of the garden; but of the tree of the knowledge of good and evil you shall not eat, for in the day that you eat of it you shall die (Gen 2:16–17).

God's Promise of a Redeemer

Even though they had sinned against him, God continued to love Adam and Eve. He wanted them, and all the human race who would descend from them, to live in his friendship. So he promised to send us a **Redeemer**, someone who would be able to reconcile us to God and restore to our souls the life of sanctifying grace. God told the devil that this Redeemer would come from a woman, saying:

I will put enmity between you and the woman, and between your seed and her seed; he shall bruise your head, and you shall bruise his heel (Gen 3:15).

Words to Know:

create body soul immortal
sanctifying grace good angels
fallen angels heaven hell
original sin Redeemer

Q. 24 *Why is God called "Creator of heaven and earth?"*
God is called "Creator of heaven and earth" because he made heaven and earth out of nothing (CCC 279, 296).

Q. 25 *Is the world entirely the work of God?*
Yes, the world is entirely the work of God (CCC 296, 299).

Q. 26 *Did God create only the material things that are in the world?*
No, God not only created the material things that are in the world, but he also created the spiritual things, such as the angels and the soul of each human being (CCC 327–28, 355).

Q. 27   *What are the pure spirits?*

The pure spirits are intelligent beings who do not have bodies (CCC 328–30, 391–93).

Q. 28   *What are the angels?*

The angels are pure spirits, invisible servants of God, and our guardians (CCC 329, 336).

Q. 29   *Do we have duties toward the angels?*

We have the duty of reverence and respect toward the angels (CCC 335).

Q. 30   *What are the demons?*

The demons were at one time angels who rebelled against God in pride and were cast into hell because of their rejection of God. They tempt man to do evil (CCC 391–94, 414).

Q. 31   *What is man?*

Man is a created reasoning being composed of body and soul (CCC 355).

Q. 32   *What is the soul?*

The soul is the spiritual part of man, by which he lives, understands, and is free. The soul makes man able to know, love, and serve God (CCC 363).

Q. 33   *What is the body?*

The body is the material part of man (CCC 364).

Q. 34   *Does man's soul die with his body?*

No, man's soul does not die with his body, it lives forever because it is a spiritual reality (CCC 1703).

Q. 35   *Why must we take care of our soul?*

We must take the greatest care of our soul because it is immortal (CCC 366–67).

Q. 36 *Does man have free will?*

Yes, man has free will because he can choose to do some thing or not do some thing, or to do one thing rather than another (CCC 1731).

Q. 37 *Who were the first human beings?*

The first human beings and our first parents were Adam and Eve (CCC 375).

Q. 38 *Was man created weak and sinful as we are now?*

No, man was not created weak and sinful as we are now, but in a state of original justice (CCC 374).

Q. 39 *What destiny did God ordain for man?*

The destiny that God ordained for man was happiness in union with God forever. Because this destiny is entirely above and beyond the capacity of human nature, man also received from God a supernatural power called grace (CCC 27, 1998).

Q. 40 *What gift did God give man in order to help him achieve his destiny?*

God gave man the supernatural gift of grace in order to help him achieve his destiny (CCC 2021).

Q. 41 *In addition to grace, what else did God give to man?*

In addition to grace, God gave man the gift of freedom from all the weaknesses and sufferings of life, including death, provided that he not sin (CCC 376).

Q. 42 *Why does man not have these supernatural gifts from God today?*

Man does not have these supernatural gifts from God today because Adam, who was the father of mankind, sinned (CCC 399, 402).

Q. 43   *What was Adam's sin?*

Adam's sin was a grave sin of pride and disobedience (CCC 397–98).

Q. 44   *What damage did the sin of Adam cause?*

The sin of Adam lost grace and every other supernatural gift for man. Adam and all men were made subject to sin, to the demons, to death, to ignorance, to evil inclinations and every other sort of suffering, and finally to exclusion from heaven (CCC 403, 405).

Q. 45   *What is the sin called to which Adam subjected the rest of mankind by his fault?*

The sin to which Adam subjected all mankind by his fault is called original sin (CCC 404).

Q. 46   *In what does original sin consist?*

Original sin consists in the loss of original grace, which God intended for us to have but was lost by Adam for all mankind (CCC 400).

Q. 47   *Did God abandon man after his sin?*

No, God did not abandon man after his sin. Because God loved man, he promised to send a Savior who would redeem man, restore the life of grace to his soul, and make it possible for him to go to heaven (CCC 410).

CHAPTER 4

God's Plan of Salvation

Sing to the LORD, all the earth! Tell of his salvation from day to day.

1 Chronicles 16:23

The beautiful story of how God prepared the world for the coming of Jesus Christ and of how Jesus accomplishes this plan for the redemption, or salvation, of the human race is called **salvation history**. Jesus was to restore the grace that had been lost through original sin.

God decided to form for himself a people, the chosen people, to whom he would reveal himself and his plan of salvation. From among this sacred community he would choose the woman who would be the mother of the Redeemer of the whole world.

God Calls Abraham

God chose a man named Abram, who lived in the land of Mesopotamia almost four thousand years ago. He made a **covenant** (agreement or promise) with him, promising to make Abram the father of many descendants, who would become a great nation. God also told him that this nation would live in a wonderful place called the **Promised Land**:

And I will make of you a great nation, and I will bless you, and make your name great, so that you will be a blessing. I will bless those who bless you, and him who

curses you I will curse; and by you all the families of the earth shall bless themselves (Gen 12:2–3).

Abram agreed to the covenant, and to show his new mission in life, God gave him the new name of Abraham, which means "father of many people." When he agreed to this covenant, Abraham showed great faith in God because he and his wife were very old and yet they believed that the Lord would give them many children. They trusted God so much that they were willing to leave family and home in order to set out for the Promised Land. The early Christians recognized the great faith that Abraham had in God; it is mentioned in the letter to the Hebrews:

By faith Abraham obeyed when he was called to go out to a place which he was to receive as an inheritance; and he went out, not knowing where he was to go (Heb 11:8).

Even today in the liturgy of the Catholic Church we honor this holy man as, "Abraham, our father in faith" (Eucharistic Prayer I).

Isaac Continues the Covenant

After God's promise of descendants, Abraham had a son named Isaac. Needless to say, the boy was loved dearly by his elderly parents. One day God wanted to test Abraham's faith. He commanded this father to sacrifice his beloved only son as an act of worship: "Take your son, your only son Isaac, whom you love, and go to the land of Moriah, and offer him there as a burnt offering upon one of the mountains of which I shall tell you" (Gen 22:2).

Knowing that man must love and serve God more than his family, Abraham took Isaac up a mountain and prepared to sacrifice him as God had commanded. Just as Abraham was about to sacrifice Isaac, an angel stopped Abraham and revealed to him that it was a test. Now God knew that Abraham truly loved him more than anyone else, and he rewarded this love by promising to continue his covenant through Isaac. After his father's death Isaac became the second **patriarch**, or leader, of God's chosen people.

The sacrifice of his only son that Abraham was willing to make was a **prefigurement** of God's love for mankind. A prefigurement is some person or event that happens before another event to which it is similar in some way. In this case, the prefigurement was of the sacrifice that God the Father was to make of allowing Jesus, his only Son, to be sacrificed on the Cross for our sins.

The Covenant Continues with Jacob

Isaac married a woman named Rebekah, and they had twin boys, Esau and Jacob. God chose Jacob as the one with whom he would keep the covenant he had made with Abraham, saying:

"I am the LORD, the God of Abraham your father and the God of Isaac; the land on which you lie I will give to you and to your descendants . . . and by you and your descendants shall all the families of the earth bless themselves. Behold, I am with you and will keep you wherever you go, and will bring you back to this land; for I will not leave you until I have done that of which I have spoken to you." (Gen 28:13–15).

Soon after this event God gave Jacob a new name, **Israel**, which means "the man who strives with God." This new name is very important because God's people used it as the name for their community: the Israelites. Jacob had twelve sons who became the fathers of the twelve tribes, or families, that made up the chosen people. Thus Jacob became the third patriarch of God's people.

The Story of Joseph

Among the many sons of Jacob, there was one who was especially dear to him—Joseph. The other sons were envious at this, and they grew angry with their brother. They began to plan among themselves how they could get rid of Joseph once and for all. One day, when they were out in the fields watching their sheep, they sold poor Joseph to a band of wandering slave traders who were on their way to Egypt. Then they told Jacob that Joseph had been

killed by a wild beast. Jacob was heartbroken. If only he knew that they had sold their brother for twenty pieces of silver!

In this, Joseph reminds us of Jesus who was sold by one of his friends for thirty pieces of silver. Joseph also prefigures Jesus because he was to become a kind of savior in Egypt for his brothers. This is how it happened.

When he arrived in Egypt, Joseph was bought by an important ruling family because he was handsome and very intelligent. Soon he became a trusted servant of the Pharaoh (the Egyptian king) and was given important positions in the royal court—he even became second in command in all of Egypt. In the meantime, the land of the chosen people was in a time of famine so the sons of Jacob travelled to Egypt in search of food. Imagine their surprise to find Joseph in command! Instead of having them killed or thrown into prison because of what they had done to him, Joseph embraced each one and gave them all the food they needed. He invited his family to move to Egypt, which they did. Joseph gave them some of the best land in Egypt and loved them with all of his heart.

In this Joseph again prefigures Jesus. Joseph forgave those who had wronged him and gave them everything they needed for a happy life. This reminds us of Christ, who forgives all of our sins and gives us every grace and blessing we need to live good Christian lives while we journey to heaven, our true home.

For four hundred years the Israelites lived in the land of Egypt. While Joseph was alive they were treated with honor and respect. The Israelites stayed in Egypt for many years and the rulers were no longer happy to have them. One particular Pharaoh made the Israelites the slaves of the Egyptian people. The descendants of Jacob were forced to do heavy manual labor from sunrise to sunset; they were used as "beasts of burden" to build many of the pyramids in Egypt. God's people soon began to think that the Lord had abandoned them; they wondered if he had taken back the wonderful covenant of blessing that he had made with Abraham, Isaac, and Jacob. It was at this difficult point in their history that God sent a very special man to his people.

Words to Know:

salvation history   covenant
patriarch   prefigurement
Promised Land   Israel

Q. 48 *What is salvation history?*

Salvation history is the fulfillment of God's saving plan in Jesus Christ to reunite man with him and share in his glory forever (CCC 430–31).

Q. 49 *From whom would be born the Redeemer of the world?*

The Redeemer of the world would be born from among God's chosen people, of a woman named Mary, who was of the house of David (CCC 488).

Q. 50 *Why is Abraham our father in faith?*

Abraham is our father in faith because he believed God's promise to make him the father of a holy people from whom our Savior was born (CCC 59–60).

Q. 51 *What is a covenant?*

A covenant is a promise or an oath that binds two people (or groups of people) together. God's covenant with the Israelites bound them to his laws so that they could know and serve him faithfully (CCC 62).

Q. 52 *Who were the Israelites?*

The Israelites were God's chosen people of the Old Testament. They were the first to hear the Word of God. God prepared them for the coming of the Savior, who would redeem the whole world (CCC 64).

CHAPTER 5

The Holy Prophet Moses

When the LORD saw that he turned aside to see, God called to him out of the bush, "Moses, Moses!" And he said, "Here am I."

Exodus 3:4

Before the coming of Jesus, the Redeemer, the most important person among God's chosen people was Moses, the first of God's prophets. He was their first leader, and he helped to make the Israelites a united people.

Moses was born in Egypt to a poor Israelite woman. At the time of his birth the Pharaoh had made a law that required the death of every newborn Israelite boy. He did this because the Jewish people were becoming a very large group, and if their numbers continued to increase they would not as easily be kept in slavery. Hoping to save the life of her son, Moses' mother hid him in a basket by the Nile River.

One day, the Pharaoh's daughter found little Moses, and she adopted him as her own son. He grew up in the royal palace and was treated as one of the family. Moses knew that he was really an Israelite by birth, and he would visit the Jewish slaves often. During one of these visits he saw an Egyptian hit one of the slaves; this filled him with so much anger that he killed the Egyptian! Realizing that he was in great trouble for having killed the Egyptian, Moses fled Egypt and went to the land of Midian. Here he became a herdsman, married a woman named Zipporah, and raised a family.

God Calls Moses

The time soon arrived when God, because of the covenant he had made with Abraham, Isaac, and Jacob, answered the prayers of his enslaved people. He appeared to Moses in a burning bush and told him to return to Egypt in order to deliver the Jews from their slavery. The Lord said to Moses:

"I have seen the affliction of my people who are in Egypt, and have heard their cry because of their taskmasters; I know their sufferings. . . . Come, I will send you to Pharaoh that you may bring forth my people, the sons of Israel, out of Egypt. . . . But I will be with you; and this shall be the sign for you, that I have sent you: when you have brought forth the people out of Egypt, you shall serve God upon this mountain" (Ex 3:7–12).

At this time God also revealed his name to Moses. He called himself **Yahweh** (Ex 3:14) which translated means, "I AM." This tells us that God is the source of all that exists; it is he alone who has the power to do all things. It also reminds us that God is *eternal*; that is, his

existence had no beginning and will have no end.

Moses Returns to the Land of Egypt

Obeying the will of God, Moses travelled to Egypt where he was accepted by the Israelites as a prophet sent from the Lord. He chose his brother, Aaron, to be his companion in God's service and they both went to Pharaoh with this message: "Thus says the LORD, the God of Israel, 'Let my people go' " (Ex 5:1).

But the Pharaoh would not think of it! Instead he increased the labor of the Jews and treated them even more harshly. In order to punish his stubbornness God sent ten plagues upon the land: water turned into blood; frogs overran the countryside; gnats, flies, and a thick dust filled the air; animals died; hailstorms descended upon the land; locusts destroyed their crops: and for three days all of Egypt was plunged into darkness. Even after all of these terrible signs, Pharaoh refused to obey the will of God in letting the Jewish people go!

The Passover of the Lord

Before sending the tenth and final plague (which was to be the death of every first-born Egyptian son and animal), God told Moses to have each Israelite family hold a special religious meal which would be a sign that they were members of his sacred people. Every family was to kill a lamb and eat it with unleavened bread and bitter herbs. They were to eat this holy meal standing, ready to leave on a journey. Before finishing this ceremony, they were to sprinkle the lamb's blood on their wooden doorposts, for this would be a signal that the home was to be spared from the tenth plague. When the angel of death went throughout the land carrying out this plague, he would *pass over* the homes of God's people. Thus the meal became known as the **Passover**. Even today, Jewish families gather together to celebrate the feast of the Passover; it is always celebrated near our Christian feast of Easter.

The Passover meal was a special preparation of God's people for Christ's saving death and for the Mass, which is the sacred sacrifice-meal of the new chosen people, the Church. Let us pause to compare these important events.

The Israelites gathered together for the Passover by the command of God; we Catholics come together every Sunday for Mass as Christ commands us. During their ceremony the Israelites sacrificed an animal known as the Paschal lamb; we offer the Father the Eucharistic sacrifice of Jesus, who is the "Lamb of God" (Jn 1:36). At the Passover meal the Israelites ate the sacrificed lamb; at every Eucharist we are invited to partake of the Body and

Blood of Jesus in Holy Communion. The Israelites sprinkled the blood of the sacrificed lamb upon the wood of their doorposts so that death would not come to them that night; at every Holy Mass the precious blood of Jesus is *sacramentally* shed for our sins so that we might be saved from eternal death (hell). Finally, because of the Passover ceremony and the tenth plague, the Israelites were freed from their slavery; because of Christ's sacrifice we are freed from slavery to sin and the devil.

Because these sacred ceremonies are so similar the liturgy of the Church for Holy Week and Easter calls the Crucifixion and the Resurrection the "**Paschal Mystery**" (Passover) of the Lord Jesus. Saint Paul, in his first letter to the Corinthians, uses this same comparison saying: "For Christ, our paschal lamb, has been sacrificed. Let us, therefore, celebrate the festival . . . with the unleavened bread of sincerity and truth" (1 Cor 5:7–8).

The Exodus from Egypt

Afraid of the power of the Israelites' God, Pharaoh let the Jews leave Egypt. We call this journey from Egypt to the Promised Land the **Exodus**. Soon after they had left the Pharaoh's city, the Egyptian ruler changed his mind and sent some of his troops to bring the Israelites back. At first God's people were terrified at seeing the soldiers coming toward them, but Moses told them to trust in the Lord. As the Israelites approached the Red Sea God intervened to save them: the mighty waters parted and there was a clear path for them to travel through! The soldiers came galloping after the Israelites, but they were too late: as soon as the last of God's people reached the other side of the sea, the waves came crashing down upon the Egyptians. You can imagine the great joy and confidence in God that filled the hearts of his people!

Even with this great sign of God's protection, the people soon grew weary of travelling in the desert where food and water were scarce. They complained to Moses: "Would that we had died by the hand of the LORD in the land of Egypt . . . for you have brought us out into this wilderness to kill this whole assembly with hunger" (Ex 16:3).

Seeking God's comfort and strength, Moses went up a mountain where he prayed to the Lord. In reply, God sent nourishment to his people in miraculous ways: he gave them a special bread called manna and water gushed forth from a rock! This bread, wondrously sent from God, prefigures the Holy Eucharist, which is the heavenly Bread of Life.

God Gives Moses the Ten Commandments

After about three months of wandering in the desert the Israelites found themselves at Mount Sinai. Moses climbed up this mountain in order to be alone for prayer. At this time God appeared to him and gave him the Ten Commandments, also called the **Law**. In the meantime the people grew weary again and complained about their situation. Many of them actually turned their backs on God saying to Aaron: "Up, make us gods, who shall go before us" (Ex 32:1).

They melted down all their gold jewelry and formed an **idol**, or image of a false god, in the shape of a calf. They worshipped this image, committing the sin known as *idolatry*. When Moses came down from Sinai he grew furious at this sin of the people. How dare they turn their backs on the one true God, the God who had made a covenant with their ancestors and who had so miraculously freed them from slavery! Moses destroyed the idol and those who had worshipped it were punished. The Israelites told God and Moses that they were sorry for having doubted. They promised to do whatever was asked of them in order to remain God's chosen people. Moses returned to Sinai in order to seek God's wisdom in this matter.

God Renews the Covenant with His People

God told Moses to give this message to the people:

> "Behold, I make a covenant. Before all your people I will do marvels, such as have not been wrought in all the earth or in any nation. . . . Observe what I command you this day" (Ex 34:10–11).

So Moses proclaimed the Ten Commandments to the people and they all answered: "All the words which the LORD has spoken we will do" (Ex 24:3).

From that day on the Commandments of the Law became the people's way of showing their loyalty to God. They considered themselves good Jews so long as they kept the Law. They had such a deep respect for the Commandments that they built a special container, called the **Ark of the Covenant**, in which the tablets of the Law were kept. They carried this with them as they journeyed to the Promised Land.

God Commands Sacrifices

As another part of the renewed covenant, God commanded that the priests of Israel offer animal sacrifices to him in worship. A **sacrifice** is the act of offering to God something that is precious to us. These gifts were to be offered on an **altar** that was **consecrated**, set apart solely for this purpose. Each time a sacrifice was offered the people would be reminded of the covenant and of their duty to obey the Law. During each sacrifice the priests would beg God to forgive the sins of all the people.

For the next few centuries of salvation history (until the perfect sacrificial death of Jesus on the Cross), these sacrifices were offered to God by the Jewish people. Thus sacrificial worship became an important religious event in the lives of the People of God.

The Israelites Enter the Promised Land

After forty years of travelling through the desert the people finally arrived in the Promised Land. However, Moses was forbidden by the Lord to enter this land because he had once doubted God's power. Even though he was a holy man and a prophet, he had to endure this punishment because he had disobeyed God's command. This shows that even one sin is "one too many" in God's eyes. Moses died just as the people were nearing the land. After burying him the Israelites entered into the land promised them from of old: the land God said he would give to Abraham, Isaac, and Jacob.

Joshua and the Judges of Israel

Joshua was Moses' successor as prophet of God and leader of the people. He was also a great warrior who led the Jews in battle against the foreigners who had taken over their land while they had been enslaved in Egypt. The book of Joshua in the Old Testament tells us about this brave man and the way he served God. Before his death, Joshua gathered the Israelites together and renewed the covenant with the Lord.

After Joshua's death there was a new kind of leadership for Israel: the judges. These were not men who presided over courts of law as our judges do; they were military heroes who won great victories for God's people. The era of the judges lasted only as long as Israel needed military men to reconquer their land. Once the community was firmly established as a nation, the work of the judges ended, and yet another new form of leadership arose: the kings.

The Rule of the Kings

At this time in salvation history there lived a holy prophet named Samuel. Since the Israelites wanted a king like all the other nations, God told Samuel to **anoint** certain men as the kings of God's people. He chose a man named Saul to be the very first king of Israel. Samuel anointed Saul king by pouring oil over his head as a sign that he had been chosen by God. Saul proved to be an unworthy king and he soon died.

His successor was David, a shepherd boy who won a mighty battle with the Philistine soldier Goliath. David became the greatest king Israel ever had; he was a strong warrior and a good government leader. Even though he committed some terrible sins he was truly sorry for them, and God forgave him. He loved God and wrote some beautiful prayers and hymns to him. We call these the **Psalms**, and even today they are used in worship. It was King David who made *Jerusalem* the capital of the Jewish nation and the center of their worship. God loved David and made a special promise to him: one of his descendants would reign as king forever! This was a prophecy about Jesus, who was a descendant of David and the true King of the Jews.

After David's death, his son Solomon became king. He was a very wise ruler who made the kingdom a good place in which to live. His words of advice were written down and can be found in some of the wisdom books of the Old Testament. Solomon had a magnificent temple built in Jerusalem; it was beautifully decorated inside with gold, fine cloth, and ornate furnishings.

Soon after Solomon's death, however, the kingdom experienced many difficulties. The Jews who lived in the northern part fought with those of the south; they eventually divided the cherished Promised Land into two separate nations. The northern kingdom was called Israel, while the southern kingdom was named Judah. It was the kingdom of Judah that remained faithful to God and to King David's policies. And it was from the people of this nation that Jesus Christ would come to us.

Words to Know:

Yahweh   Passover   Paschal Mystery
Exodus   Law   idol
Ark of the Covenant   sacrifice   altar
consecrated   anoint   Psalms

The Ten Commandments of God

1. I, the Lord, am your God. You shall not have other gods besides me.
2. You shall not take the name of the Lord, your God, in vain.
3. Remember to keep holy the sabbath day.
4. Honor your father and mother.
5. You shall not kill.
6. You shall not commit adultery.
7. You shall not steal.
8. You shall not bear false witness against your neighbor.
9. You shall not covet your neighbor's wife.
10. You shall not covet anything that belongs to your neighbor.

Q. 53   *Who was Moses?*

Moses was a great prophet in the Old Testament, through whom God established his covenant with the Israelites and gave them the Ten Commandments (CCC 62).

Q. 54   *What was the Passover?*

The Passover was the great event of the liberation of Israel from slavery in Egypt (CCC 1334).

Q. 55   *What are the Ten Commandments?*

The Ten Commandments are the moral laws that God gave to Moses on Mount Sinai and which Jesus Christ perfected in the New Testament (CCC 2056).

CHAPTER 6

God's Special Spokesmen: The Prophets

For this is he who was spoken of by the prophet Isaiah when he said, "The voice of one crying in the wilderness: Prepare the way of the Lord, make his paths straight."

Matthew 3:3

In our study of salvation history we have seen that men called **prophets** have played an important role in the dealings which God had with the Jews. Many people misunderstand what a prophet is. Most think that it means a person who foretells future events in strange and mysterious ways. While it is true that part of a prophet's mission may be to tell us about future events, this is not the main purpose of these holy men. A prophet is someone chosen by God to speak a message from God to the people. Usually this message is about their present concerns, something that they need to hear for their spiritual well-being. The prophet speaks these words with the authority, or permission and power, of the Lord.

The Mission of the Prophets in Israel

God sent many such men to his people. They were sent to remind the Jews about the covenant by which they were bound to God. The prophets told the people to be faithful to the Law and to refuse to worship false gods as their pagan neighbors did. By doing these things the prophets were really preparing the Jews for the coming of the **Messiah**, a name which means "the Anointed One." In Greek the word for "Anointed One" is *Christos*, from which we get "Christ." As we learned in the previous chapter, "anointed" means someone chosen by God for a special role; in this case, the Anointed One is the Redeemer whom God promised to send to the human race, Jesus Christ.

The prophets encouraged the people to trust in God, not in the powerful nations of the earth, for peace and protection. They warned them that God would punish them if they did not live as his holy people, observing the Commandments of the Law.

The Prophets Proclaimed God's Message in Many Ways

The prophets delivered the Lord's messages in many ways. They spoke the words, put them into poetry, and sometimes even acted them out in little skits! They were so devoted to God and to their mission that they used any method they could to get the people to hear God's Word and obey it.

41

The Different Kinds of Prophets

The spokesmen of God whom we know most about are those whose **prophecies** (messages from God) and lives are recorded in the Old Testament. They are divided into two groups: the major and the minor prophets.

The major prophets are those who wrote a lot; their names are Isaiah, Jeremiah, Ezekiel, and Daniel. The minor prophets, whose writings are not as abundant, are Hosea, Joel, Amos, Obadiah, Jonah, Micah, Nahum, Habakkuk, Zephaniah, Haggai, Zechariah, and Malachi.

The Prophets Elijah and Elisha

There are two very great prophets who are not included in the above lists because they did not leave us any of their writings. But their lives are recorded in the Bible and they are very important in salvation history. Their names are Elijah and Elisha. Elijah, who was always considered the greatest prophet of them all, was very devoted to God. He is most famous for a contest he held with some pagan priests on Mount Carmel. He wanted to prove to the people that the God of the Israelites was the one true God, so he told the pagan priests to set up altars of sacrifice and ask their gods to set these altars on fire. Of course no matter how long they prayed nothing happened. However, when Elijah set up his altar, he flooded it with water and asked God to set it on fire. Behold! a blaze came down from heaven and consumed the animal that was on it! Elijah's holiness drew many men to him; they wanted to serve God too.

The most important of Elijah's followers was Elisha. He lived with the holy prophet Elijah and saw him taken up into heaven in a fiery chariot (2 Kings 2:11). Elisha continued serving God with the same love and devotion that had filled the heart of his master, Elijah. He worked many miracles, one of which was multiplying bread for the hungry, just as Our Lord did centuries later.

Elijah and Elisha are especially important to the Catholic Church because one of its greatest religious orders, the Carmelites, owes its existence to the disciples of these prophets. The priests, brothers, nuns, and lay people who belong to the Carmelite Order dedicate their lives to offering prayers and sacrifices to God for the needs of his people, just as the holy prophets had done centuries ago.

The Prophet Isaiah

A most important prophet for Christians is Isaiah, who lived eight hundred years before the birth of Christ. More than the others, Isaiah spoke about the coming Messiah. Here are some of his prophecies about the Redeemer:

The Messiah's virgin mother: "Behold, a young woman shall conceive and bear a son, and shall call his name Immanuel" (Is 7:14).

The Messiah will be a great light: "The people who walked in darkness have seen a great light; those who dwelt in a land of deep darkness, on them has light shined" (Is 9:2).

The Messiah will be a great ruler: "For to us a child is born, to us a son is given; and the government will be upon his shoulder, and his name will be called 'Wonderful Counselor, Mighty God, Everlasting Father, Prince of Peace.' Of the increase of his government and of peace there will be no end" (Is 9:6–7).

The Messiah will suffer: "Surely he has borne our griefs and carried our sorrows; yet we esteemed him stricken, smitten by God, and afflicted. But he was wounded for our transgressions, he was bruised for our iniquities; upon him was the chastisement that made us whole, and with his stripes we are healed" (Is 53:4–5).

The Messiah shines in glory upon the people: "Arise, shine; for your light has come, and the glory of the LORD has risen upon you. . . . And nations shall come to your light, and kings to the brightness of your rising" (Is 60:1, 3).

We use these and other prophecies about the Messiah from Isaiah in our Advent and Christmas liturgies in the Catholic Church.

Saint John the Baptist, Herald of the Messiah

The last of the Old Testament prophets and the only one who is present in the New Testament is Saint John the Baptist. He was a "bridge" between these two parts of salvation history, and it was his privileged mission to prepare the Jews for the public ministry of Our Lord.

John was born only six months before Jesus, and he was Our Lord's cousin (his mother was Mary's relative). His parents, Zechariah and Elizabeth, were elderly and had no children. They wanted a baby so badly! One day, when Zechariah was in the temple worshipping God, an angel appeared to him with this happy message:

"Do not be afraid, Zechariah, for your prayer is heard, and your wife Elizabeth will bear you a son, and you shall call his name John. And you will have joy and gladness, and many will rejoice at his birth, for he will be great before the Lord (Lk 1:13–15).

At John's birth the Holy Spirit inspired his father with wonderful words about the little boy. He revealed to Zechariah that John was to be the **forerunner** and **herald** of the Messiah. A forerunner is someone who goes before another person to prepare the people for his coming; a herald is someone who announces the coming of a royal person. The Holy Spirit gave Zechariah these words about John:

And you, child, will be called the prophet of the Most High; for you will go before the Lord to prepare his ways, to give knowledge of salvation to his people in the forgiveness of their sins (Lk 1:76–77).

When John grew up he began his mission in the area around the Jordan River, not far from the city of Jerusalem. He would tell the people to **repent** (to give up their sinful desires and actions). John is called the "Baptist" (or the Baptizer) because he would pour water upon those people who wanted to give up sin, as a sign of their desire to repent. He would often say to the crowds that came to him: "I baptize you with water; but he who is mightier than I is coming . . . he will baptize you with the Holy Spirit and with fire" (Lk 3:16).

John was speaking of Jesus, who was soon to make his appearance among the people. Like all of the other prophets sent by God, John was a victim of persecution. King Herod, who was living a sinful and impure life, did not like to hear John say that his actions were wrong. He had the Baptist thrown into prison and later sentenced him to be beheaded.

John did not care that he was to die, for he had finished the work that was his to do. He had faithfully prepared the people for Jesus' preaching, and he was ready to meet death with a loyal heart. Saint John the Baptist is one of the most important saints of the Church, and, after Our Lady, he receives the most honor in the Church's prayers and liturgy.

Words to Know:

prophets   Messiah   prophecies
forerunner   herald   repent

Q. 56   *Who were the prophets?*
The prophets were God's servants who prepared his people for the coming of the Messiah by calling for repentance from sin and faithfulness to God (CCC 64).

Q. 57   *What does "Messiah" mean?*
The word "Messiah" is the Hebrew word for "Anointed One" and refers to the one who is anointed by the Holy Spirit as the Savior of God's people (CCC 436).

Q. 58   *Who was the last and greatest of all the prophets?*
Saint John the Baptist was the last and greatest of the prophets because he prepared the way of the Lord Jesus (CCC 523).

PART TWO

God
Becomes Man

CHAPTER 7

Our Lord and Savior Jesus Christ

*And the Word became flesh and dwelt among us, full of grace and truth;
we have beheld his glory, glory as of the only Son from the Father.*

John 1:14

You will remember that God promised Adam and Eve that he would send a Redeemer, someone who would make up for original sin and the separation it caused between man and the Creator. We have seen how God began his plan for our salvation by choosing a community of people, the Jews or Israelites, to whom he gradually revealed his plan. He sent prophets to these people to prepare them for the coming of the Messiah, the "Anointed One" of God.

The various prophets had told the Jewish people that the Messiah would indeed come to them, but they never said exactly *who* he would be. Most of the people expected a great and powerful military leader who would free them from political oppression. That this Savior would be God himself, come down to liberate them from their spiritual slavery to sin and the devil, was not what they expected.

But the prophets did give the people some clues about the Messiah, ways to recognize him once he came. They said that he would be a member of the tribe of Judah (Gen 49:8–10); he would be born of a virgin (Is 7:14) in the town of Bethlehem (Micah 5:2–4). A great star would shine in the sky to announce the Mes-

siah's birth (Num 24:17), and he would live for a time in Egypt (Hos 11:1). This Redeemer would preach God's good news to the poor and the lowly (Is 61:1–3), but he would be rejected by the people who would cause him much suffering (Is 53:1–12).

You probably recognize the life of the Lord Jesus in the above prophecies; many of the Jews did, and they accepted him as the Messiah sent from God. But many others did not.

The Incarnation of Our Lord

From among all the women of the chosen people, God selected one through whom he would fulfill his promise of salvation: the Virgin Mary of Nazareth. God had prepared her to cooperate with his plan of salvation. Mary was free from original sin from the moment of her conception. This is called the Immaculate Conception. One day, he sent the angel Gabriel to her, saying:

> Hail, full of grace, the Lord is with you!
> . . . Do not be afraid, Mary, for you have found favor with God. And behold, you

will conceive in your womb and bear a son, and you shall call his name Jesus. He will be great, and will be called the Son of the Most High; and the Lord God will give to him the throne of his father [ancestor] David, and he will reign over the house of Jacob for ever; and of his Kingdom there will be no end (Lk 1:28, 30–33).

Now Mary, as the Church has always taught, was a virgin, as her response to this angelic messenger reveals: "How can this be, since I have no husband?" (Lk 1:34).

The angel told her that God, in his almighty power, would work this great wonder within her. By the power of the Holy Spirit the child would be conceived in her womb. Joseph, to whom she was betrothed, would *seem* to be the baby's father but he was actually the Lord's foster father and protector. Mary, ready to do whatever God asked of her, replied to the angel: "Behold, I am the handmaid of the Lord; let it be to me according to your word" (Lk 1:38).

With these words Mary showed how dedicated she was to God's plan for her life and for our salvation. She called herself the "handmaid" of the Lord, which is another way of saying that she was God's servant or slave, ever ready to do whatever he asked of her.

As soon as Mary expressed her consent to God's will, Jesus was conceived in her womb; this is the virginal conception. Nine months later he was born in the little town of Bethlehem, and his **nativity** (birth) was announced by the appearance of the miraculous star, just as had been foretold. We call the event by which the Son of God took on our human nature the **Incarnation.**

The Divinity of Jesus

The Second Person of the Holy Trinity came down from heaven in order to share our human life. Even more, he freely chose to be born in poverty and to live a poor life, so that we could learn that wealth and worldly pleasures do not give us true happiness. He became man so that we, by being freed from sin and reunited with God by Baptism, could become like him, the children of the Father. Saint Irenaeus, a holy bishop of the second century, once said: "The Word of God, Jesus Christ, on account of his great love for mankind, became what we are in order to make us what he is himself."

For thirty years Jesus lived a normal human life with Mary and Joseph, working as a carpenter in the village of Nazareth. He did this in order to teach us that even such ordinary things as work and family life are very important to God. This first part of Christ's life is called his "hidden life," because during this time the people did not know *who* he really was and because we do not know very much about it.

When Our Lord was about thirty years old he began what is known as his "public life," that is, the three years he spent preaching, teaching, and working miracles. These **miracles** were signs and proofs of his divinity; they showed that he was truly the Son of God. A miracle is some event or happening that is beyond the powers of man or of nature. It can only be worked by God, who is the Lord and Master of all creation.

The public life of Jesus began with his baptism in the Jordan River by Saint John the Baptist. At this time, the **evangelists** (writers of the Gospels) tell us that the Holy Spirit came down upon Jesus and the Father's voice was heard to say: "This is my beloved Son, with whom I am well pleased" (Mt 3:17).

This was the first time that Jesus of Nazareth was publicly revealed as the Son of God. (Of course, Mary and Joseph already knew who he was.) It was also the first time that the mystery of the Holy Trinity was revealed. During his ministry Our Lord spoke of himself as the Son of God, saying: "Truly, truly, I say to you, before Abraham was, I am" (Jn 8:58). (Remember that "I AM" is the name God revealed to Moses in the burning bush.)

So we see from all of these events recorded for us in the Gospels that Jesus Christ is *both* God and man at the same time! This is a great mystery of faith, but we accept it because God has revealed it. We call this mystery the **hypostatic union**. This phrase comes from a Greek word which tells us that Our Lord is the Son of God and the son of Mary, fully God with all of the divine powers, and fully man like us in everything except sin.

The Humanity of Jesus

Jesus had everything that makes someone a human being: a physical body with all of its various functions, and an immortal soul with its powers of intellect and will. As a man he had to grow daily in acquiring human knowledge, and he experienced the joys and sorrows of life just as we do. The Gospels remind us that he felt hunger and thirst (Lk 4:2); he loved children (Mk 10:13–16); he knew sorrow and cried over the death of a friend (Jn 11:32–36); he experienced loneliness (Mt 26:37–46); he enjoyed friendship (Lk 19:1–10); felt joy and gladness (Lk 10:21); he went through suffering and death (the accounts of the Passion in all four Gospels).

We noted that Jesus was like us in all things except sin (Heb 4:15). This is because, as the Second Person of the Holy Trinity, he is all-holy. But this does not mean that Jesus was free from temptations to sin; the Gospels make it very clear that he was tempted (Mt 4:1; Mk 1:13; Lk 4:2–13). Since he was a human being like us, this means that we too can live free from sin, with the help of his grace which is always available to us through the sacraments. Jesus has made it possible for us to live a sinless life just as he did!

Errors about the Incarnation

Throughout the history of Christianity **heresies**, or errors, about the mystery of the Incarnation have been taught by various mistaken followers of the Lord. Heresies are very dangerous to the faith because they corrupt or destroy man's understanding of the truth which leads to salvation.

The first heresy to attack the truths taught by the Church happened in the days of the apostles of the Lord; it was called **Docetism**. It corrupted the truth that Jesus is human. This heresy said that Christ only *seemed* to be a man. Some people believed this because they viewed the human body as evil; so naturally, according to their way of thinking, God would not take on a real human body! The Magisterium of the Church condemned these teachings of the Docetists as heresy, and Saint John wrote his Gospel partly to show that the Docetists were wrong. But this heresy lives on in our own day among those who think that the human body is sinful and not something which God created as good. It also affects those Christians who see Christ only as the Son of God, and not as a true, full human being.

Another terrible heresy sprang up among Christians in the beginning of the fourth century. It was started by a priest who denied the truth about Christ's divinity. The priest's name was Arius, and so his false teaching was called **Arianism**. Arians believed that Our Lord was the Messiah sent from God, that he was the greatest of teachers and holiest of men, but they did not believe that he was divine. An unfortunate thing about this heresy is that it attracted thousands of Christians, including many bishops! We can learn from this that even priests and bishops can be led astray from the Gospel if they do not remain united to the Pope, for at that time the Holy Father and a few faithful bishops were the only ones teaching the truth about Jesus' divinity. As you can well imagine, things got so out of hand that the first **ecumenical council** (meeting of all the bishops of the Church in union with the Pope) was held in order to condemn this false teaching officially. It is called the Council of Nicea (A.D. 325), and from this meeting we received the **Nicene Creed**, which we recite every Sunday at Holy Mass.

Unfortunately, Arianism can still be found today among those who call Christ a "great man" and "moral leader" but who refuse to acknowledge his full divinity. These people place Jesus on the same level as the founders of other religions (such as Buddha or Mohammed), and consider Christianity to be simply one religion among all the others. They fail to see that God has become man for them, for all of us, so that we can truly live with him on this earth and forever in heaven.

Words to Know:

nativity   Incarnation   miracles
evangelists   hypostatic union
heresies   Docetism   Arianism
ecumenical council   Nicene Creed

Q. 59   *What was the Annunciation?*
The Annunciation was the holy event of the angel Gabriel announcing to Mary that she was to be the mother of the Messiah, Jesus, the Son of God (CCC 494).

Q. 60   *Who is Jesus Christ?*
Jesus Christ, the Second Person of the Holy Trinity, is the Son of God made man in the Incarnation (CCC 461).

Q. 61   *How was the Son of God made man?*
The Son of God was made man by the power of the Holy Spirit in the pure womb of the Virgin Mary (CCC 497).

Q. 62   *From whom was Jesus Christ born?*
Jesus Christ was born of Mary, ever-virgin, who is therefore the Mother of God (CCC 495).

Q. 63   *Who is the father of Jesus Christ?*
God is the father of Jesus Christ (CCC 496, 502).

Q. 64   *Who was Saint Joseph?*
Saint Joseph was the foster father and guardian of Jesus, and the spouse of Mary (CCC 497).

Q. 65   *Did the Son of God cease to be God when he was made man?*
When the Son of God was made man he did not cease to be God, but while remaining true God, he became true man (CCC 469, 479).

Q. 66   *Are there two natures in Jesus Christ?*
Yes, in Jesus Christ there are two natures: divine and human (CCC 470, 481).

Q. 67   *With the two natures in Jesus Christ are there also two persons?*
With the two natures in Jesus Christ there are not two persons, but only one, the Divine Person of the Son of God, the Second Person of the Holy Trinity (CCC 468, 481).

Q. 68   *Did Jesus Christ always exist?*
Jesus Christ has always existed as God; he began to exist as man from the moment of the Incarnation (CCC 479).

Q. 69   *Where was Jesus Christ born?*
Jesus Christ was born in a stable at Bethlehem (CCC 525).

CHAPTER 8

The Saving Mission of Jesus

But when the time had fully come, God sent forth his Son, born of woman, born under the law, to redeem those who were under the law, so that we might receive adoption as sons.

Galatians 4:4–5

The Father sent his only Son into our world for the salvation of the human race. Saint John the Apostle proclaimed this saving mission of Jesus and reminds us that it was the Father's will, his plan, for his Son:

> For God so loved the world that he gave his only Son, that whoever believes in him should not perish but have eternal life. For God sent the Son into the world, not to condemn the world, but that the world might be saved through him (Jn 3:16–17).

Jesus and the Father

Jesus always had his mind set on the Father, whom he loved with all his heart. He showed this deep love by faithfully doing the **will of God**, even if this meant suffering and hardship as in his Agony in the Garden or his death upon the Cross.

Our Lord often spoke of his oneness with the Father. One day, after having multiplied bread for the hungry, Jesus said: "For I have come down from heaven, not to do my own will, but the will of him who sent me" (Jn 6:38).

At many other times during his life Christ revealed the intimate relationship which he enjoyed with his Father:

> The Father loves the Son, and has given all things into his hand (Jn 3:35).
> For this reason the Father loves me, because I lay down my life, that I may take it again (Jn 10:17).
> I do as the Father has commanded me, so that the world may know that I love the Father (Jn 14:31).
> I am not alone, for the Father is with me (Jn 16:32).

We see from these words that Jesus did everything out of love for God and in obedience to his will. Nothing which the Father asked of him was too much or too difficult, for Jesus' love knew no limits.

Prophet, Priest, and King

The Father sent Jesus to be his greatest Prophet, the teacher of God's truth. He was also sent to be our Priest, who offered himself in sacrifice to the Father, and our King, who came to start the Kingdom of God upon earth. We call these three roles of Christ his **triple office** or three-fold office.

Jesus Our Teacher

Jesus the Prophet, or Teacher, helps us to reach heaven by telling us how to live lives that are pleasing in God's sight. Only in Jesus' teachings do we find the way that leads to heaven. Jesus said of himself: "I am the way, and the truth, and the life; no one comes to the Father, but by me" (Jn 14:6).

By his words and example Jesus told us about the Father's great love for us; he revealed that the Father had sent him as our Savior, the One who would take away our sins. We call this the **good news** of our salvation.

Jesus shared his role as Teacher with his followers. He teaches us today through the Magisterium (teaching office) of the Catholic Church. This duty to share the faith with others is also a very important part of every Christian's life. By Baptism and Confirmation we are called to spread the faith to others by our words, good example, and apostolic effort.

Jesus Our Priest

Jesus is our one true Priest whose sacrifice on the Cross won for us the gift of *sanctifying grace*, which, as we learned in our study of man's creation, is the life of God in our souls. In order to make this life of grace available to all men of every time and place, Jesus gave us the sacraments and told his apostles to bring these holy gifts to all the world. This is the role of the ministerial priesthood.

Every Christian shares in the common priesthood of Jesus through the anointing received at Baptism and Confirmation. This means that we are set apart from other men and women as the true worshippers of God. **Worship** is the prayer and adoration which we offer to God, especially through the Mass and sacraments. We can also worship God privately in many ways, for example, by making acts of *faith, hope*, and *love*.

Jesus Our King

Even before his birth the Messiah was called the great king or ruler of God's people. The angel Gabriel had revealed to Mary: "The Lord God will give to him the throne of his father David, and he will reign over the house of Jacob for ever; and of his kingdom there will be no end" (Lk 1:32–33).

The Jews thought that the Messiah would be the ruler of an earthly kingdom, but Jesus corrected this mistaken view, saying: "My kingship is not of this world; if my kingship were of this world, my servants would fight, that I might not be handed over to the Jews; but my kingship is not from the world" (Jn 18:36).

Our Lord meant that his Kingdom is spiritual. Everyone who lives in the state of sanctifying grace belongs to the Kingdom of Christ, which is the Church. The **Kingdom of God** (also called the Kingdom of Heaven or the Reign of God) is the greatest place for a person to live. We live in it on earth by faithful membership in the Church, and we will live in it in heaven for ever. It is so wonderful that Jesus used to tell a **parable**, or story, in which his Kingdom is compared to a treasure and to a pearl (Mt 13:44–46). He said that the person who discovers this treasure will see its value and give up anything that stands in the way of obtaining it.

The "thing" that usually stands in our way of having the treasure of God's Kingdom is sin. For this reason Jesus gave us the sacraments of Baptism and Penance; through these sacred ceremonies we are freed from sin and made holy members of his Kingdom. According to the parable, if we really value the Kingdom we will give up sin so that this pearl and treasure will be ours forever.

Words to Know:
will of God   triple office   good news
worship   Kingdom of God   parable

Q. 70   *What is the triple office of Jesus?*
The triple office of Jesus is that of prophet, priest, and king (CCC 436).

CHAPTER 9

The Priesthood of Jesus

Although he was a Son, he learned obedience through what he suffered; and being made perfect he became the source of eternal salvation to all who obey him, being designated by God a high priest after the order of Melchizedek.

Hebrews 5:8–10

In the last chapter we learned that one of Jesus' roles as the Savior was to be our Priest. This meant that he was to offer the Father a perfect sacrifice for our sins. Because this is a most important part of our salvation we will look more closely at the priesthood of Jesus in this chapter.

Offering Sacrifices to God

We have seen that the idea of offering sacrifices to God has been part of salvation history since the days of the Exodus. But it really goes all the way back to Cain and Abel, the sons of Adam and Eve.

The first sacrifices mentioned in the Bible were those of these two brothers:

> In the course of time Cain brought to the LORD an offering of the fruit of the ground, and Abel brought of the firstlings of his flock and of their fat portions. And the LORD had regard for Abel and his offering, but for Cain and his offering he had no regard. So Cain was very angry, and his countenance fell (Gen 4:3–5).

This story goes on to tell us that God had accepted Abel's offering because he had a pure heart, while Cain's heart was full of jealousy toward his brother.

The Bible also tells us that Noah offered an animal on an altar to God, thanking him for having spared his family during the great flood and acknowledging God to be Lord and Creator of the earth.

The book of Leviticus, in the Old Testament, has to do with the offering of sacrifices to

> The LORD has sworn and will not change his mind, "You are a priest for ever after the order of Melchizedek."
>
> (Psalm 110:4)

God; it tells us that these sacrifices were commanded by God as a way of showing sorrow for sin. Through these offerings the chosen people hoped to obtain forgiveness.

We learn from the Bible three very important things about offering sacrifices to God:

1. The gift must be offered with a pure or sinless heart.

2. The offering is a thanksgiving to God for his blessings and protection.

3. The offering of sacrifices shows sorrow for sin and a desire for forgiveness.

These Old Testament accounts of sacrifice also remind us that three things are required for every offering:

1. a **priest**, that is, someone to do the offering. In the Jewish nation God himself selected certain men to be his priests.

2. a **victim**, that is, something to be offered. God told the Jews to offer certain animals, especially the Passover lamb.

3. an **altar**, that is, somewhere for this offering to take place. For the Jewish priests the altars of sacrifice were located in the temple.

Jesus Our Sinless High Priest

All of the Jewish sacrifices were but a preparation for the one perfect sacrifice that Jesus was to offer to God. He is called our High Priest, which means that he is the greatest priest of God. Why? Because he was sinless, the Son of God, who came down from heaven in order to give perfect worship to the Father. The other priests were but imperfect men who could not worship God with sinless hearts.

Jesus Our Sinless Victim

Along with being the Priest of his sacrifice, Jesus was also the Victim. His altar, or place of offering, was the table of the Last Supper and the Cross of Calvary: two different places but only one Priest, one Victim, and one Sacrifice.

At the Last Supper Jesus the perfect Priest offered himself to the Father under the appearances of bread and wine. He had changed these into himself with the words, "This is my Body. . . . This is my Blood." Thus the perfect Victim was being offered.

The words, ". . . is given for you . . . is poured out for you" (Lk 22:19–20), tell us two things: that Jesus is offering a sacrifice to God for our sakes and that this Sacrifice of the Eucharist is connected to that of his Crucifixion, which happened the next day.

On Mount Calvary, the place where Jesus was crucified, the same sacrifice-offering to the Father was made. As with the Last Supper, Jesus was the Priest who offered himself. He was the Victim, but this time it was a bloody, painful offering. By his death, which the Lord offered *for us*, the one true sacrifice for sin was finally given to God. Unlike the animals offered by the Jewish priests, this sacrifice *worked!* It indeed made up for every sin and reconciled us to the Father!

How can we be sure? Because the Resurrection took place. This showed that God had accepted the sacrifice of his Son. We no longer need to wonder about it—Jesus was freed from the grip of death as the sign that we, too, are freed from death and its cause: sin. The great

Saint Paul wrote about this in his letters to the Colossians and the Corinthians:

> He has now reconciled [you] in his body of flesh by his death, in order to present you holy and blameless and irreproachable before him (Col 1:22).

> If Christ has not been raised, your faith is futile and you are still in your sins (1 Cor 15:17).

Jesus Our One Mediator

Besides the offering of sacrifice the priest had the duty of praying for his people, asking God to look upon their offering and to forgive their sins. This is called *mediation*, and the priest is a "go-between," or **mediator**.

As man Jesus is our one, perfect mediator. His wounds from the Crucifixion are no longer painful and bloody, but they are glorious reminders to the Father of his sacrifice. Also as man, he prays to the Father for us. He shows the wounds of the Crucifixion, now glorious, to the Father to remind him of his one perfect sacrifice that took away our sins. Saint Paul revealed this truth of Jesus as our mediator to his friend and fellow bishop, Saint Timothy: "For there is one God, and there is one mediator between God and men, the man Christ Jesus" (1 Tim 2:5).

A Priest Like Melchizedek

Christ's priesthood is foretold in the Old Testament: "The LORD has sworn, and will not change his mind, 'You are a priest for ever after the order of Melchizedek'" (Ps 110:4).

Who was Melchizedek and how is he connected to Jesus' priesthood? He was a king of Salem (later called Jerusalem) and a priest who offered *bread and wine* to God in sacrifice. Saint Paul tells us that this is why he is compared to Jesus. No one else had offered the gifts

of bread and wine, before Christ. Even today, at the *ordination* ceremonies of Catholic priests, the verse from Psalm 110 is used as one of the prayers for the Mass.

Words to Know:

priest victim altar mediator

57

Q. 71 *How is the sacrifice of Christ on the Cross a perfect Sacrifice?*

The sacrifice of Christ on the Cross is a perfect sacrifice because he is the perfect Priest who offered himself as the perfect Victim in obedience and love for the salvation of man (CCC 2100).

Q. 72 *When was the Sacrifice of Christ offered?*

The Sacrifice of Christ was offered at the Last Supper and fulfilled on the Cross, in one and the same Sacrifice to the Father (CCC 1340).

Q. 73 *How does the Sacrifice of Christ continue today?*

The Sacrifice of Christ continues today as the Holy Eucharist, in which Christ's Body and Blood are offered for the forgiveness of sins (CCC 1365–67).

CHAPTER 10

Christ, Source of All Grace

They are justified by his grace as a gift, through the redemption which
is in Christ Jesus, whom God put forward as an expiation by his blood,
to be received by faith. This was to show God's righteousness, because
in his divine forbearance he had passed over former sins.

Romans 3:24–25

The Son of God became man so that we might receive the gift of God's life of grace that our first parents had lost for us. We call him the **Source of All Grace**, the One from whom we receive this wonderful gift of God's life in our souls.

Saint John the Apostle reminds us of this truth: "And the Word became flesh and dwelt among us, full of grace and truth. . . . And from his fulness have we all received, grace upon grace" (Jn 1:14, 16).

Sanctifying grace is God's greatest gift to us. It makes us the children of the Father, brothers and sisters of Jesus Christ, and temples of the Holy Spirit. Those who die with this life of God in their souls go to heaven, where they enjoy never-ending happiness with the Holy Trinity, Mary, and all the angels and saints. Nothing else in the entire universe can do this for us. Now you can see why Jesus would consider grace to be something important enough to die for.

Jesus' Mission of Grace

Whenever God gives a mission to someone he also gives him everything he will need to carry it out. He never asks the impossible of anyone. The Incarnation (God the Son becoming man) gave Jesus of Nazareth all that he needed to carry out his mission. By being both God and man, Our Lord was totally filled with grace. All of his actions were perfect and holy because they were the actions of God the Son and not simply those of a good human being.

Because he was God as well as man, Jesus had supernatural powers which made it possible for him to **redeem** us, that is, to free us from our slavery to sin and the devil. The four Gospels are full of true stories that reveal Christ's power over sin and satan:

He could expel evil spirits or devils from possessed people:

> And immediately there was in their synagogue a man with an unclean spirit; and he cried out, "What have you to do with us, Jesus of Nazareth? Have you come to destroy us? I know who you are, the Holy One of God." But Jesus rebuked him, saying, "Be silent, and come out of him!" And the unclean spirit, convulsing him and crying with a loud voice, came out of him (Mk 1:23–26).

He worked miracles and taught with an authority that amazed the people:

> And they were all amazed, so that they questioned among themselves, saying, "What is this? A new teaching! With authority he commands even the unclean spirits, and they obey him." And at once his fame spread everywhere throughout all the surrounding region of Galilee (Mk 1:27–28).

He gave proof that he could forgive sins:

> And many were gathered together, so that there was no longer room for them, not even about the door; and he was preaching the word to them. And they came, bringing to him a paralytic carried by four men. And when they could not get near him because of the crowd, they removed the roof above him; and when they had made an opening, they let down the pallet on which the paralytic lay. And when Jesus saw their faith, he said to the paralytic, "My son, your sins are forgiven. . . . But that you may know that the Son of man has authority on earth to forgive sins"—he said to the paralytic—"I say to you, rise, take up your pallet and go home." And he rose, and immediately took up the pallet and went out before them all; so that they were all amazed and glorified God, saying, "We never saw anything like this!" (Mk 2:2–12).

Jesus Gives Grace to All Men

Jesus fulfilled his mission. He won for us the grace of redemption, which means that whoever believes in him can live a new life, one that is blessed with God's friendship and that will last forever. We first receive this new life in Baptism, and grow in it through prayer and reception of the other sacraments.

Jesus entrusted these sacraments to his Church, which is the Kingdom of God upon earth. Through the prayers and preaching of his priests Jesus continues to defeat Satan and to conquer sin. Through his priests he continues to give the grace of God to all those who believe.

This new life of grace has been made possible for us *only* by the life, death, and Resurrection of Jesus Christ, the Source of All Grace, "from whom all good things come" (Eucharistic Prayer III).

Because without Jesus we would have no grace and because Jesus was conceived and born of the Virgin Mary, she is often called the **Mediatrix**, or channel, of all grace.

Words to Know:
Source of All Grace   redeem   Mediatrix

Q. 74   *What is heaven?*

Heaven is the perfect and everlasting life of love and happiness with the Holy Trinity, the Virgin Mary, the saints, and the angels (CCC 1024).

Q. 75   *Who may go to heaven?*

Those who die in God's friendship and grace and are perfectly purified will live with God forever in heaven (CCC 1023).

Q. 76   *How was the life of grace won?*

The life of grace was won by Jesus' suffering, death, and Resurrection (CCC 654).

Q. 77   *How can man receive God's life of grace and grow in it?*

Man can receive God's life of grace through faith and Baptism, and he grows in it through prayer, acts of charity, and reception of the sacraments (CCC 1693–66, 1692).

CHAPTER 11

Jesus Founds His Church

So with yourselves; since you are eager for manifestations of the Spirit, strive to excel in building up the church.

1 Corinthians 14:12

We have seen that an important part of salvation history was the forming of a people, God's *chosen people*, to whom divine revelation was given and from whom the Messiah would come. They were very proud of this gift from God. But Saint Paul tells us that most of the Israelites rejected the Messiah when he came; he just did not meet their idea of what the Anointed One should be. But those Jews who accepted Jesus as Lord and who put their faith in him became the *new* chosen people of God. By their acceptance of Our Lord they remained faithful to their calling as God's chosen ones.

Jesus Calls the Twelve Apostles

When Jesus was about thirty years old he began preaching the good news of the Kingdom of God. He gathered around himself a small band of followers to whom he carefully taught his message of salvation. These men became known as the **twelve apostles** and they were the foundation members of the new People of God, the Church. Saint Mark tells us about this important event:

And he went up into the hills, and called to him those whom he desired; and they came to him. And he appointed

twelve, to be with him, and to be sent out to preach and have authority to cast out demons: Simon whom he surnamed Peter; James the son of Zebedee and John the brother of James, whom he surnamed Boanerges, that is, sons of thunder; Andrew, and Philip, and Bartholomew, and Matthew, and Thomas, and James the son of Alphaeus, and Thaddaeus, and Simon the Cananaean, and Judas Iscariot, who betrayed him. Then he went home (Mk 3:13–19).

The choice of *twelve* leading members of this new community was very meaningful to the Jews. In the Old Testament you will remember that the Israelites were made up of twelve tribes coming from the twelve sons of Jacob. Jesus chose twelve apostles to show that his Church was the continuation of the chosen people.

Jesus Makes Simon Peter The Head of His Church

Our Lord knew that he was soon to leave our world and return to his Father. To make sure that his Church would have a supreme leader, one who would be his own representative on earth, Jesus chose Simon. Just as God had given Abraham and Jacob new names to go with their new missions, so Jesus gave Simon the new name of Peter (which means "rock") to show that he had a new mission in the Church:

> Simon Peter replied, "You are the Christ, the Son of the living God." And Jesus answered him, "Blessed are you, Simon Bar-Jona! For flesh and blood has not revealed this to you, but my Father who is in heaven. And I tell you, you are Peter, and on this rock I will build my church, and the powers of death shall not prevail against it. I will give you the keys of the kingdom of heaven, and whatever you bind on earth shall be bound in heaven, and whatever you loose on earth shall be loosed in heaven" (Mt 16:16–19).

The other apostles and the early Christians all recognized Peter as the head of all the apostles and of the Church: what we now call the **Pope** (Pope means "father"). They knew that Jesus had appointed him to this position of unique leadership. They listened to Peter and obeyed his decisions, just as they had done to Jesus. They considered Peter's voice to be the voice of Christ to them.

Jesus Gives the Apostles His Authority

Along with Peter, Jesus prepared the other apostles for their roles of leadership in his Church. He shared his authority with all of them, giving them special spiritual gifts that would help them carry out the mission of teaching, ruling, and sanctifying (making holy) the new People of God.

They were to nourish Jesus' followers by giving them his Body and Blood in the Eucharist: "This is my body. . . . This cup is the new covenant in my blood. . . ." (1 Cor 11:24–25).

The apostles were to be Christ's voice in the world, teaching the good news to all nations: "He who hears you hears me, and he who rejects you rejects me, and he who rejects me rejects him who sent me" (Lk 10:16).

They were to make rules that would protect the goodness of the Christian way of life: "Truly, I say to you, whatever you bind on earth shall be bound in heaven, and whatever you loose on earth shall be loosed in heaven" (Mt 18:18).

They were to help the Christians to become holy by forgiving their sins: "If you forgive the sins of any, they are forgiven; if you retain the sins of any, they are retained" (Jn 20:23).

They were to be his special witnesses whom the Holy Spirit would send out to all the world: "But you shall receive power when the Holy Spirit has come upon you; and you shall be my witnesses in Jerusalem and in all Judea and Samaria and to the end of the earth" (Acts 1:8).

By giving these responsibilities to the apostles, Jesus made them the chief shepherds of his Christian flock. He made them the first **bishops** of the Church.

The Church of Jesus Christ

There are many ways of looking at the Church in order to understand her importance in our lives. There are some images of the Church that Jesus himself used. He called her a sheepfold or flock of which he is the Good Shepherd (Jn 10:1–18). He also said that the Church was like a grapevine; he is the main vine and we are the branches (Jn 15:1–8). Our Lord often compared the Church with a kingdom, calling her the Kingdom of God or the Kingdom of Heaven. This tells us that in the Church, God is the highest authority and we are to be his loyal subjects, ever ready to do the King's will.

As a visible organization led by the Pope and the bishops in union with him, the Church is called a **hierarchy**, which means a sacred order. This way of ordering the Church reminds us that Jesus gave his authority to the Church so that she could be his true voice in the world. It also reminds us that we must obey these chosen leaders as we would Jesus himself. The order of membership in this structure is Pope, bishops, priests, and lay people.

Another way of looking at the new community of God is to see it as the **pilgrim Church**. This reminds us that we are traveling toward heaven. Life on earth is a spiritual journey that will be finished when we reach heaven. Some of us arrive at our destination sooner than others, but at the end of the world the entire community of the faithful will be there forever!

Seeing the Church as a continuation of Israel, we call her the new chosen **People of God**. This tells us that everyone, from the Pope to the littlest child, is a member of this community. Saint Peter wrote about this image in his first letter to all the Christians of the world:

> But you are a chosen race, a royal priesthood, a holy nation, God's own people, that you may declare the wonderful deeds of him who called you out of darkness into his marvelous light (1 Pet 2:9).

Saint Paul reminds us that the Church is the **Mystical Body of Christ**. He compared her to a human body with a head and many other parts, or members. Christ is the head of the Church. As the head of the body directs and unifies the parts of the body, so Christ directs and unites the members of his Church. The Church lives from Christ and in Christ. The Church lives for Christ. And Christ lives with and in his Church by his Spirit. The image of the Church as a body helps us to remember that we may have different roles in the Church, but we all must work together to bring the good news of Jesus to the world. A foot cannot work without a leg, and a head cannot function without the other body parts. If one member sins all the others are hurt by it. Sometimes you hear a person say that he can do whatever he wants as long as no one gets hurt. Well, this simply is not true for Christians. As Saint Paul says:

> If one member suffers, all suffer together; if one member is honored, all rejoice together. Now you are the body of Christ and individually members of it (1 Cor 12:26–27).

Finally, Saint Paul taught that the Church is the Bride of Christ and that Christ is the Bridegroom of the Church. Jesus and his Church are so close to each other that they are like a husband and wife in marriage. Christ loves the Church as a husband loves his wife. The Church should love Christ as a wife loves her husband.

Another way of understanding the Church can be found in the Apostles' Creed: the **Communion of Saints**. This name reminds us that the Church's membership can be found in three places: heaven, purgatory, and earth. In heaven she is called the *Church Triumphant* because the members have reached man's spiritual goal and are crowned with victory. In purgatory she is called the *Church Suffering* because the members are being purified of imperfections before they can enter heaven. On earth she is called the *Church Militant* because we have to fight against sin as we try to remain faithful to Jesus.

The Marks of Christ's Church

There are hundreds of Christian denominations today, and many of them claim to be the true Church founded by the Lord. How can we know which church is really and fully his? There are four *marks*, or signs, that show us that the Catholic Church was founded by Christ. These **four marks of the Church** can be found in the ancient Nicene Creed that we recite at Mass: "We believe in *one, holy, catholic*, and *apostolic* Church."

The Church of Christ is ONE. Catholics share *one faith, one Baptism, one head* on earth (the Pope), and *one Sacrifice* of the Mass.

> There is one body and one Spirit, just as you were called to the one hope that belongs to your call, one Lord, one faith, one baptism (Eph 4:4–5).

The Church of Christ is HOLY. She was founded by Jesus who is all-holy. He died so that all her members could become holy by believing his holy doctrines and receiving his holy sacraments.

> Christ loved the church and gave himself up for her, that he might sanctify her, having cleansed her by the washing of water with the word, that he might present the church to himself in splendor, without spot or wrinkle or any such thing, that she might be holy and without blemish (Eph 5:25–27).

The Church of Christ is CATHOLIC. This is from a Greek word meaning "universal" and it shows us that only the Catholic Church teaches all men of every age the whole gospel of Christ. It is this mark that gave the Church of Jesus her name.

> And Jesus came and said to them, "All authority in heaven and on earth has been given to me. Go therefore and make disciples of all nations, baptizing them in the name of the Father and of the Son and of the Holy Spirit, teaching them to observe all that I have commanded you; and

lo, I am with you always, to the close of the age" (Mt 28:18–20).

The Church of Christ is APOSTOLIC. Her beginnings go back through time to the days of the apostles of the Lord. "So then you are no longer strangers and sojourners, but you are fellow citizens with the saints and members of the household of God, built upon the foundation of the apostles" (Eph 2:19–20). Only the Catholic Church can fully make this claim. The Eastern Orthodox church, which separated from the Catholic Church in the eleventh century retained apostolic succession, but without recognizing the primacy of the Pope. Protestantism, which did not retain apostolic succession, began in the sixteenth century.

Only the Catholic Church is one, holy, catholic, and apostolic in the way that the Church founded by Christ was. The Church of Christ, then, exists fully in the Catholic Church alone. That does not mean that other Christians are cut off from Christ or are in no way related to the Church he founded. Christians who are not Catholic share much of our Faith. They have many elements of holiness and truth. All Christians accept the Bible as God's word and believe in Jesus as Our Savior. All Christians who truly believe in Jesus possess the same Holy Spirit. We can even say that they have a certain imperfect unity with the Catholic Church, so long as they do not knowingly and deliberately reject the Catholic Church. Even so, Jesus does not want his followers to remain divided. We should pray that one day all Christians will be united in the fullness of the Catholic Church.

Words to Know:
twelve apostles   Pope   bishops
hierarchy   pilgrim Church
People of God   Mystical Body of Christ
Communion of Saints
four marks of the Church

Q. 78   What is the Church?
The Church is the community of disciples, who, through the Holy Spirit, profess the faith of Jesus Christ, participate in his sacraments, and are united in communion with the pastors he has appointed (CCC 815).

Q. 79   Who founded the Church?
The Church was founded by Jesus Christ, who, by the Holy Spirit, united his followers into one community, under the direction of the apostles, with Saint Peter as their head (CCC 763–66).

Q. 80   Why did Jesus Christ institute the Church?
Jesus Christ instituted the Church so that men might have in her a secure guide and the means of holiness and eternal salvation (CCC 775–76).

Q. 81 *Where do we find the Church of Jesus Christ?*
The Church of Jesus Christ continues to exist fully in the Catholic Church alone because she alone is one, holy, catholic, and apostolic in the way which Jesus Christ himself willed the Church to be (CCC 811).

Q. 82 *How is the Church one?*
The Church is one in her origin from God; in her founder Jesus Christ; and in her life of the Holy Spirit; and also one in her faith, in the sacraments, and in her pastors (CCC 813, 815).

Q. 83 *How is the Church holy?*
The Church is holy through her founder Jesus Christ and his Holy Spirit, as well as though her holy faith, her sacraments, and the obedience of her members as manifested in the Saints (CCC 823).

Q. 84 *How is the Church catholic?*
The Church is catholic, or universal, in that she was instituted for all men, is suitable for all men, and has extended over the whole world (CCC 836).

Q. 85 *How is the Church apostolic?*
The Church is apostolic in that she was founded on the apostles and continues in their teaching, sacraments, and authority, though their successors, the bishops (CCC 857).

Q. 86 *Who are the chief pastors of the Church?*
The chief pastors of the Church are the Pope and the bishops in union with him (CCC 862, 880).

Q. 87 *Who is the Pope?*
The Pope is the Successor of Saint Peter, the bishop of Rome, the visible head of the Church, and the Vicar of Jesus Christ, who is the invisible head of the Church (CCC 881).

CHAPTER 12

The Church in Our Time

"... teaching them to observe all that I have commanded you; and lo, I am with you always, to the close of the age."

Matthew 28:20

After the Ascension of the Lord into heaven, the apostles returned to their dwelling in Jerusalem. Saint Luke tells us that they spent nine days in prayer with Mary, the Mother of Jesus, and some other disciples. On the tenth day, the feast of **Pentecost**, the Holy Spirit, whom Christ had promised to send, came down upon all present in the forms of fire and wind. This was the birthday of the Church; the Kingdom of God now began to live and spread throughout the earth, with Peter and the apostles as its leaders. Saint Luke tells us about this historic day:

> When the day of Pentecost had come, they were all together in one place. And suddenly a sound came from heaven like the rush of a mighty wind, and it filled all the house where they were sitting. And there appeared to them tongues as of fire, distributed and resting on each one of them. And they were all filled with the Holy Spirit and began to speak in other tongues, as the Spirit gave them utterance (Acts 2:1–4).

The Holy Spirit transformed the apostles. Until then they had been afraid to preach about Jesus for fear that they, too, would be killed by the people. But now they were bold and full of courage! They went out into the streets of Jerusalem proclaiming the truth about Jesus as Son of God and Messiah. That day alone they brought three thousand people into the newborn Church!

The Church Spreads throughout the World

After a while the twelve apostles divided up the various parts of the known world among themselves. They went out to all the nations, preaching the gospel, baptizing new Christians, ordaining new bishops and priests, celebrating Holy Mass, and starting communities of believers wherever they went.

Peter, the Pope, went to Rome and to this day his successors still live and serve there. We cannot be completely sure where some of the other apostles went, because the New Testament does not say. But according to very ancient tradition Andrew went to Greece and Russia; James the Greater (John's brother) served in Spain, but later returned to Jerusalem where he became the first apostle to die as a **martyr** for the Lord. Philip preached in Asia Minor while James the Less became the first bishop of Jerusalem. Bartholomew went to Armenia and Thomas to India. Matthew served in the many communities of Palestine where he wrote his Gospel. Thaddaeus, also called Jude, went with Simon the Zealot to Iran and its surrounding countries. Matthias, who took the place of Judas the traitor, preached in Ethiopia. John, who was the youngest of them all, took care of Our Lady and eventually died in Turkey. He wrote a Gospel, three letters, and the book of Revelation before he died. All of these holy men, except for John, died as martyrs. Their heroic deaths were a final way of telling us that the life, death, and Resurrection of Jesus were *true*.

From the various communities founded by these apostles and by Saint Paul, who was called to be an apostle by the Risen Jesus, the Church grew and grew. Some of the other followers of Our Lord brought the faith to France and Britain. Many centuries later Spanish, Portuguese, and French missionaries brought

the faith to the Americas. Today the Catholic Church can be found in every country, carrying on Christ's work of salvation.

The Spirit's Gifts to the Church

In order to make this apostolic and missionary work possible, the Holy Spirit has given the Catholic Church two very special gifts: infallibility and indefectibility. They are long words for two very simple things.

Infallibility means that the Church is kept free from error in teaching us about faith and morals. Jesus had promised this gift to the Church when he said at the Last Supper:

> And I will pray the Father, and he will give you another Counselor, to be with you for ever, even the Spirit of truth, whom the world cannot receive, because it neither sees him nor knows him; you know him, for he dwells with you, and will be in you. . . . But the Counselor, the Holy Spirit, whom the Father will send in my name, he will teach you all things, and bring to your remembrance all that I have said to you (Jn 14:16–17, 26).

This gift of infallibility was given to protect the message of salvation that Jesus had given to his Church. The Pope alone, or the Catholic bishops of the world teaching in union with the Pope, can make use of this gift since they are the official teachers of the Church.

Indefectibility means that the Church will be present on earth until the end of the world. Our Lord made this promise twice. The first time was when he made Peter head of the Church: he had said that not even the "powers of death" would destroy his Church (Mt 16:18). The second time was as at the Ascension. He said to the apostles: "I am with you always, to the close of the age" (Mt 28:20).

This gift of indefectibility also means that

the mission of the Church will never change. The Church will always be the sure voice of Jesus in the world, spreading his gospel and administering his sacraments. She will always have a pope and bishops; she will always teach the truth in every age.

The Catholic Church has outlasted many civilizations. She survived the destruction of Jerusalem in A.D. 70. She endured through three hundred years of persecution by the Roman Empire and saw that empire collapse. She has continued on through the attacks of thousands of enemies and terrible heresies. Catholics in recent centuries have been victims of hatred by many governments and are persecuted even today. But the Church remembers that Jesus had foretold all of this at the Last Supper, saying: "If the world hates you, know that it has hated me before it hated you. . . . [B]ut be of good cheer, I have overcome the world" (Jn 15:18, 16:33).

The Church Brings Jesus to Every Age

With the help of these two wonderful gifts, the Church brings Jesus and his good news to people in every century. While the teaching of the Church remains the same, some of her rules and ways of worshipping can differ or change. This enables the Church to present the message of Jesus to people of various cultures in a way that is understandable to them.

For example, the Holy Mass is celebrated by Catholics in different ways, called **rites**. Most Catholics belong to a rite called the Roman rite because our ceremonies come from the diocese of Rome. The Mass you attend at your parish is probably celebrated according to this rite. You are one of the followers of Christ known as **Roman Catholics**. The second largest group of Catholics belong to the Byzantine rite; they are called **Byzantine Catholics**. Their way of offering Mass is different from ours and their churches are decorated in a very different way. But they are members of the true Church just as we are. We all look to the same Lord Jesus and the same Pope for guidance and direction as we journey to heaven.

Another way in which the Church can change with the times is by changing some of her rules according to the needs of her members. Of course she can only change some rules, not all of them, and certainly not those which have been given to us by God. For example our Sunday Mass obligation can now be fulfilled on Saturday evening. The Church did not always allow this. But since a significant number of people were unable to go to Mass on Sunday because of work or other serious obligations the Church judged it best to change that rule.

The Church does not change because she is "tired" of being the same all the time. She only changes rules or ways of worship so that she can be all things to all men—"I have become all things to all men, that I might by all means save some" (1 Cor 9:22).

Words to Know:
Pentecost   infallibility
indefectibility   rites
Roman Catholics   Byzantine Catholics

Q. 88   *Who is the Holy Spirit?*

The Holy Spirit is God, the Third Person of the Holy Trinity, the Sanctifier of souls (CCC 691, 703).

Q. 89   *Who sent the Holy Spirit for the life of the Church?*

The Father and the Son sent the Holy Spirit for the life of the Church (CCC 245–46).

Q. 90   *What is Pentecost?*

Pentecost is the event of the descent of the Holy Spirit upon Mary and the apostles fifty days after Easter. It is the birthday of the Church (CCC 731, 737).

Q. 91   *What do the Pope and the bishops united with him constitute?*

The Pope and the bishops united with him constitute the teaching body of the Church, called the Magisterium (CCC 888–89).

Q. 92   *Can the Pope and the bishops united with him err in teaching the truths revealed by God?*

The Pope and the bishops united with him cannot err in teaching the truths revealed by God because the Spirit of Truth assists them in teaching (CCC 889).

Q. 93   *Can the Pope acting alone err in teaching the truths revealed by God?*

The Pope acting alone cannot err in teaching the truths revealed by God because the Spirit of Truth assists him (CCC 891).

PART THREE

God Shares His Life

CHAPTER 13

Doctrine of Grace

If the Spirit of him who raised Jesus from the dead dwells in you, he who raised Christ Jesus from the dead will give life to your mortal bodies also through his Spirit who dwells in you.

Romans 8:11

We have learned that God created each one of us to know, love, and serve him on earth, and to live with him forever in heaven. This is the purpose of our lives. So it must be very important that we learn *how* to do these things as best we can.

But this is an impossible task for us. How can we, who have been separated from God because of original sin, reach the greatness of heaven? We cannot! That is, we cannot unless God comes to our help with his **grace**.

Grace is a supernatural gift from God given to us through Jesus Christ. It is called **supernatural** because it is far above our natural human powers. It is even above the powers of God's greatest creatures, the mighty angels! It is called a free *gift* because it is something we do not have a right to and something we cannot merit on our own. God gives it to us simply because he loves us.

God's Greatest Gift: Sanctifying Grace

Because of original sin all of us are conceived without the gift of grace in our souls. There have been only two exceptions: Jesus, who being God was always full of grace, and

his mother Mary, who received grace at the moment of her conception in her mother's womb.

Sanctifying grace makes us holy and pleasing to God; it makes us his adopted children and temples of the Holy Spirit. It gives us the right to live in heaven. This is why it is called God's greatest gift to us. There is only one thing that can ever take this gift away from us: mortal sin.

Sanctifying grace gives us a share in God's life. There are different kinds of life in the world. A living tree has *plant life* by which it can grow, blossom, and bear fruit. A dog has *animal life* that makes it better than a tree. It can see, hear, and move about. People have *human life* that allows us to think, to love, and to communicate ideas. But God's life which comes to us through grace is the greatest of them all, for with it we can live in heaven. Without it we cannot.

Along with giving us a share in God's life, sanctifying grace gives us three supernatural powers: faith, hope, and charity. We will learn about these three powers in the next chapter.

We receive sanctifying grace in the seven sacraments of the Church. Baptism first gives this new life to our souls and Confirmation

strengthens it. The other sacraments, especially the Holy Eucharist, deepen this life of God. Penance gives it back to us if we have lost it by mortal sin. Anointing prepares us for physical and spiritual healing or the grace of a happy death.

The Gift of Actual Grace

Another kind of grace gives us all of the day-to-day helps that we need in order to do good and avoid evil. **Actual graces** come to us in the form of inspirations that enlighten our minds or move our wills. Some examples of actual graces are the desire to pray or to read the Bible, and the urge to help someone who is sick or who needs help with homework. Whenever we say "yes" to these desires and carry out the good works they suggest, we become better Christians and more pleasing to God.

Without the help of actual graces we could not avoid sin or do good works for others. These graces help us to treat other people with respect and show us the way to live a good Christian life.

Words to Know:

grace   supernatural
sanctifying grace   actual grace

76

Q. 94 *What is sanctifying grace?*

Sanctifying grace is a supernatural gift which abides in our soul and makes us holy, children of God, and heirs of heaven (CCC 1999).

Q. 95 *If sanctifying grace is lost by mortal sin, how can it be restored?*

Sanctifying grace lost by mortal sin can be restored by receiving the Sacrament of Penance (CCC 1468).

Q. 96 *Is sanctifying grace necessary to go to heaven?*

Yes, sanctifying grace is necessary to go to heaven (CCC 1023).

CHAPTER 14

Faith, Hope, and Charity

Make love your aim, and earnestly desire the spiritual gifts, especially that you may prophesy.

1 Corinthians 14:1

The previous chapter helped us to learn that grace, especially sanctifying grace, is God's most wonderful gift to the Christian. It fills us with God's life, making us his adopted sons and daughters. It makes us holy temples of the Spirit, who comes to live in our souls. When the Spirit comes to us he brings three virtues that help us to believe, trust, and love God. These are called the virtues of faith, hope, and charity.

A **virtue** is a permanent power that helps us to do good and avoid evil. It can be either natural (something we work for, such as the virtue or power to be honest) or supernatural

(given directly by God without our having to work for it). Faith, hope, and charity are supernatural virtues given to our souls at Baptism along with sanctifying grace. These three powers are also called **theological virtues**. The word "theological" means "of God," so this name reminds us that faith, hope, and charity come from God and are meant to help us live for God.

Whoever is in the state of sanctifying grace (that is, a person who is baptized and has not lost this grace by mortal sin) has these powers. But they are like muscles of the soul that need to be strengthened by exercise if they are to be in good shape and useful to us. The way we exercise these spiritual muscles is by good works and by prayer, especially the *acts of faith, hope*, and *charity*. You will find prayers for making these acts at the end of this book.

Let us now look at each of these virtues and see how they help us to live the Christian life.

The Power of Faith

With the virtue of **faith** we receive the power to *believe in God* and in all that he has revealed through Christ and the Church. Faith helps us to see how all-good, all-loving, and all-truthful God is. It helps move us to give ourselves to him completely. Without faith, we would never be able to believe in God or in the revelation he has given us. Thus, we see right away that faith is necessary for salvation; it makes us *just*, or holy, in the sight of God as Saint Paul reminded the Christians in Rome: "Therefore, since we are justified by faith, we have peace with God through our Lord Jesus Christ" (Rom 5:1).

There is a big difference between *believing* something and *understanding* something. The power of faith makes it possible for us to believe what God has revealed. This means that we say "yes" to the truth even if we do not fully understand it. For example, a judge or a jury believes the testimony of a witness in court. They were not present at the scene of the accident or crime but the witness was. They accept his word as true. We were not present during Christ's life but the apostles were. Through the supernatural virtue of faith we accept their testimony as true—that Jesus worked great miracles and rose from the dead. And God blesses this faith which we have in his Son, in his apostles, and in the Church: "Blessed are those who have not seen and yet believe" (Jn 20:29).

For our faith to be true and pleasing to God it must be:

1. Firm: We must place all our faith in God whom we know could never deceive us or lead us astray.

2. Complete: We must accept all that God has revealed, not simply "picking and choosing" from among Our Lord's teachings.

The Power of Hope

The virtue of **hope** makes it possible for Christians to *trust in God*. It helps us to find comfort in Jesus' promise of eternal life: "I am the resurrection and the life; he who believes in me, though he die, yet shall he live, and whoever lives and believes in me shall never die" (Jn 11:25–26). Hope has to do with things that seem impossible, such as salvation. Do you remember when Jesus said how hard it would be for a rich man to enter heaven and the disciples asked him who could then be saved (Mt 19:24–25)? Well, Jesus' response to his disciples shows us what hope really means. He said, "With men this is impossible, but with God all things are possible" (Mt 19:26). Hope tells us that God, who promised heaven to us, will give us all the strength we need to get there. He is faithful to his word, so we can put our trust in him.

The Power of Charity

Charity (also called love) is the greatest of the three supernatural virtues, as Saint Paul told the Christians of Corinth:

So faith, hope, love abide, these three; but the greatest of these is love (1 Cor 13:13).

Charity is the power by which we *love God above all things and our neighbor as ourselves.* You will remember that Jesus called this the greatest commandment of God. It has such a high place of honor because it is the bond of friendship between God and man. Saint John, often called the "Apostle of Love," told us that by charity God dwells in our souls: "God is love, and he who abides in love abides in God, and God abides in him" (1 Jn 4:16).

But what is love? Some people think that it means *feeling* good about someone or something. They are very wrong! While it is true that we might feel good about someone we love, this is not what love means. True love means that we want only what is really good for the person. To love God means that we want to please him by doing good and avoiding sin. To love our neighbors means that we want good things for them, especially that they reach heaven. This is why Jesus told us that we must not wish evil things for others, not even our enemies (Mt 5:43–48)!

Words to Know:

virtue   theological virtues
faith   hope   charity

Q. 97   *What is a virtue?*
A virtue is an abiding habit to do good (CCC 1803).

Q. 98   *What are the two kinds of virtues?*
The two kinds of virtues are natural virtues, which are aquired by repeating naturally good acts, and supernatural virtues which come to us only as gifts of God (CCC 1804, 1812–13).

Q. 99   *What are the virtues proper to the Christian?*
The virtues proper to the Christian are the theological virtues (CCC 1812).

Q. 100   *What are the theological virtues?*
The theological virtues, which have God as their motive and object, are faith, hope, and charity (CCC 1812–13).

Q. 101   *How do we receive the theological virtues?*
We receive the theological virtues through sanctifying grace by means of the sacraments (CCC 1266).

Q. 102   *Which is the most excellent among the theological virtues?*
The most excellent among the theological virtues is charity because it unites us intimately to God and to our neighbor (CCC 1826–27).

Q. 103   *What is faith?*
Faith is the theological virtue by which we believe God and all that he has revealed, as it is proposed by the Church (CCC 1814).

Q. 104   *What is hope?*
Hope is the theological virtue by which we trust God and rely on him to provide what is necessary to obey him and to merit eternal life (CCC 1817).

Q. 105 *What is charity?*

Charity is the theological virtue by which we love God above all things for his own sake and love our neighbor as ourselves because we love God (CCC 1822).

Q. 106 *Why should we love God for his own sake?*

We should love God for his own sake because he is supremely good and the source of every good thing we have (CCC 1844, 2055).

Q. 107 *Why must we love our neighbor?*

We must love our neighbor because it is God's commandment that we love one another as he has loved us (CCC 1823).

Q. 108 *Are we obliged to love our enemies?*

Yes, we are obliged to love our enemies, forgiving them any offense, because they are also our neighbors (CCC 1825, 2303).

FAITH　　　**HOPE**　　　**CHARITY**

CHAPTER 15

The Cardinal Virtues

For this very reason make every effort to supplement your faith with virtue, and virtue with knowledge.

2 Peter 1:5

Once we have received the gift of sanctifying grace we may not simply "sit back" and believe that we are saved. God calls each one of us to *prove* our love for him by growing in prayer and good works. A most important way of showing our love is by living the *virtues*.

As we learned in the previous chapter, a virtue is a permanent power that we have which helps us to do good and avoid evil. Faith, hope, and charity are supernatural virtues given to us by God. There are other virtues that we must acquire by practice. The four main ones are prudence, justice, temperance, and fortitude. They are called the **cardinal virtues** because all of our good actions depend or "hinge" upon them. ("Cardinal" comes from a Latin word meaning "a hinge.")

These four powers are the foundation of a good life. By practicing them we become *virtuous* and are strengthened to do great things out of love for God and neighbor.

The Virtue of Prudence

Prudence is the ability to make the right choices in life. Many times we find ourselves in very difficult situations. We are not sure what Christ would do if he were in our shoes. Well, prudence shows us the way; it "tells" us

what to do in order to be faithful to Jesus.

Saint Maria Goretti was a twelve-year-old girl who lived on a farm near Rome. One summer day, in July 1903, she was murdered by a teenage boy. This young man had wanted Maria to commit a sin against purity with him; he held a knife against her, ready to kill her if she refused. Prudence told Maria that the right thing to do was to scream for help while trying to get away from the attacker. She knew that death was a very real possibility, but she also knew that mortal sin was even worse. No one heard Maria's screams as she was being stabbed. She died the next morning after having forgiven and prayed for her attacker.

Today, Maria is honored throughout the world as a martyr of purity. Prudence showed her the right way—the way that leads to heaven.

The Virtue of Justice

Justice is the virtue which helps us to live honestly by respecting the rights of others. The just person gives to everyone what he deserves. To God he gives worship; to his parents, respect and obedience; to his friends, charity and loyalty. Jesus spoke to us about justice when he said: "So whatever you wish that men would do to you, do so to them; for this is the law and the prophets" (Mt 7:12).

The unjust person thinks only about his own needs and desires. Pontius Pilate, the leader of the Romans in Palestine, was unjust to Our Lord. When Jesus was brought before him in trial he knew that Christ was innocent. But he also knew that the leaders of the Jews wanted Jesus dead and that it would ruin his political career if he went against their wishes. Thinking only about himself, Pilate condemned Our Lord to Crucifixion. He followed the wrong desires of the crowd instead of doing what was right and good.

The Virtue of Temperance

Temperance is the power to control ourselves. We usually think of it only as having to do with food or drink, but temperance helps us in every situation.

Saint Dominic Savio was an Italian teenager who lived in the middle of the 1800s. He went to a Catholic high school where he soon became the most popular boy in his class. Everyone wanted to be with Dominic because he was so cheerful and good-hearted. After he died at fifteen years of age from a painful illness, a great secret was discovered about Dominic: he had promised God that he would never commit even *one* mortal sin!

Dominic's confessor told the other boys that he had kept his promise, and these friends wondered how Dominic had done it. They all knew from experience how difficult it was to do good and avoid sin. They found out from their friend's confessor (who was a saint himself: John Bosco) that Dominic was able to keep his promise because of temperance. He never overate, never overslept, never overdid anything. By keeping control over his physical needs Dominic had learned to control his selfish desires too.

The Virtue of Fortitude

Fortitude is the virtue that helps us to face every difficulty or danger with inner peace and courage. It allows us to carry out our duties even if doing so might require great sacrifice and suffering.

All of the holy martyrs of the Church showed fortitude when they chose to remain loyal to Jesus, even though this meant being thrown to the lions or being killed in other terrible ways. Fortitude did not make it easy or take away their fears, but it strengthened them to do what was right no matter what.

There is one young martyr we should all know about. His name is Saint Pancras, and he was only fourteen when he died in the year 304. Pancras was a very handsome boy and so strong that he always beat the other teenagers in wrestling matches. One day, he won a match against a young pagan boy who was very vain and conceited. To get even, this boy revealed to the Emperor that Pancras was a Catholic. This was forbidden by Roman law.

The Emperor had been a good friend of Pancras' dead father and he wanted to spare the boy. He tried to get him to change his mind. "Just offer some prayers to our gods," the Emperor said, "and I will give you power in the

Empire." But Pancras, even though afraid of being killed, refused to deny Jesus. He replied, "By Baptism I am a son of God. I can never give up Jesus Christ, not even for an empire!"

So Pancras was condemned to death. What a courageous teenager he was, as he was led through the streets like a criminal. He did not cry out while the soldiers whipped him, nor did he change his mind as he heard the crowds joke about him. Instead he thought about Jesus being led through the streets of Jerusalem to his Crucifixion. Before he was killed by the sword, Pancras said this prayer which showed his inner peace and fortitude:

> Thank you, Lord Jesus, for the suffering I am about to receive. I accept it with joy, knowing that my death will bring me to heaven to be with you forever. My God, save those who are about to kill me!

We do not have to be martyrs to practice such fortitude! We all have to be strong as we try to live as Christians in a world that does not think much of our holy way of life. We all have to remain loyal to Jesus when students in our class want us to go out drinking or do other things that are wrong for a teenager. And each one of us can have the same peace and joy that filled Saint Pancras by loving Jesus more than anything else.

Practice Makes Perfect

Just as virtues are habits of doing good, and they strengthen God's life in the soul, man can also have habits of doing wrong actions. These bad habits are called vices, which weaken God's life in the soul and can lead us to sin. There are seven principal vices (also known as *cardinal sins*): pride, avarice, lust, anger, gluttony, envy, and sloth. We can overcome these vices by practicing their opposing virtues: humility, liberality, chastity, patience, sobriety, brotherliness, and diligence in the service of God (respectively). Both vices and virtues are habits, so we must make an effort to overcome our bad habits (vices) and grow in good habits (virtue). Practice makes perfect! If you want some guidance as to how you can grow in virtue, you may read the lives of saints or ask your parish priest. Your parish priest can show you ways to do this; simply ask him the next time you go to confession.

By living the virtuous life we will be happy. Jesus assured us of this happiness in his Sermon on the Mount when he promised it to those who live the Christian life. That life is summed up in the **beatitudes**.

Words to Know:

cardinal virtues prudence justice
temperance fortitude beatitudes

"Put on then, as God's chosen ones, holy and beloved, compassion, kindness, lowliness, meekness, and patience, forbearing one another and, if one has a complaint against another, forgiving each other; as the Lord has forgiven you, so you also must forgive. And above all these put on love, which binds everything together in perfect harmony. And let the peace of Christ rule in your hearts, to which indeed you were called in the one body. And be thankful."   (Colossians 3:12–15)

The Beatitudes

Blessed are the poor in spirit, for theirs is the kingdom of heaven.

Blessed are those who mourn, for they shall be comforted.

Blessed are the meek, for they shall inherit the earth.

Blessed are those who hunger and thirst for righteousness, for they shall be satisfied.

Blessed are the merciful, for they shall obtain mercy.

Blessed are the pure in heart, for they shall see God.

Blessed are the peacemakers, for they shall be called sons of God.

Blessed are those who are persecuted for righteousness' sake, for theirs is the kingdom of heaven.

Blessed are you when men revile you and persecute you and utter all kinds of evil against you falsely on my account. Rejoice and be glad, for your reward is great in heaven.

Mt 5:3–12

Q. 109 *What is a moral virtue?*

A moral virtue is a habit of doing good, acquired by repeatedly doing good acts (CCC 1803–04).

Q. 110 *What are the principal moral virtues?*

The principal moral virtues are: religion, by which we give God the worship owed to him, and the four cardinal virtues: prudence, justice, fortitude, and temperance (CCC 1804).

Q. 111 *What is the virtue of prudence?*

Prudence is the virtue that helps us to judge what is truly good and to choose the right means of attaining it (CCC 1806).

Q. 112 *What is the virtue of justice?*

Justice is the virtue by which we give each one what is due to him (CCC 1807).

Q. 113 *What is the virtue of fortitude?*

Fortitude is the virtue by which we hold firm in pursuing the good, despite difficulty or dangers (CCC 1808).

Q. 114 *What is the virtue of temperance?*

Temperance is the virtue by which we control our passions and desires (CCC 1809).

Q. 115 *What are the passions?*

The passions are strong emotions which must be moderated by reason and will in order to do good and avoid evil (CCC 1763–66).

Q. 116 *Where did Jesus Christ sum up the virtues of the Christian life?*

Jesus Christ summed up the virtues of the Christian life in the beatitudes (CCC 1716).

Q. 117 *What is a vice?*

Vice is a habit of doing evil, acquired by repeating bad actions (CCC 1865).

Q. 118 *What are the principle vices?*

The principal vices are the seven capital sins of pride, avarice, envy, wrath, lust, gluttony, and sloth (CCC 1866).

CHAPTER 16

The Seven Sacraments

For the grace of God has appeared for the salvation of all men.

Titus 2:11

We know that Adam and Eve lost the gift of grace for all mankind by their disobedience to God's commands. God sent his only Son to bring grace back to the world. How? By dying on the Cross as a sacrifice for our sins, a sacrifice accepted by the Father, who raised Jesus from the dead.

But this raises an important question: How did Jesus plan to give this grace to us, to every person who will ever live? The New Testament and Sacred Tradition give us the answer: Jesus gave us the seven sacraments as the ways to receive the grace of God.

What Is a Sacrament?

The **sacraments** are seven visible signs, or ceremonies, that were instituted (given) by Christ to give us grace. They must not be thought of as "magical rites" that give grace as a vending machine would give soda pop! They are sacred ceremonies in which we are truly called by Jesus to accept his love and forgiveness, and to grow in our relationship with him and with the whole Church, with our brothers and sisters in Christ.

Each of the sacraments has special words (the form) and actions or things (the matter) that bear a message for us. We are all familiar

with signs that are meant to give us a message. For example, when we see the flag of the United States, we know that it represents that country. We all understand a smile to be a message of joy, while tears are most often a message of sorrow. Words are verbal **signs**. For example, if I say the word "dog" to you, you understand it as a message about a four-legged furry animal that barks.

The Signs of the Sacraments

The signs of the sacraments bring us their own special messages too. For example, the sign of Baptism tells us that someone is being freed from original sin and being made a child of God. The sign of the Holy Eucharist tells us that bread and wine are being changed into the Body and Blood of Jesus. Once we learn what the signs are, it is quite easy to remember what each of the sacraments does for our souls.

But unlike ordinary human signs, the sacraments received power from Jesus to *do* what they tell us. This can be quite confusing so let us look at it a little more closely. Consider the ordinary *stop sign*. Whenever we see this red eight-sided sign we stop at an intersection because this is what it reminds us to do. But it does not have the power to make us stop;

we must do that ourselves. If the stop sign had the power of a sacrament, it would be able to make us stop as soon as we saw it. This is difficult to understand because the sacraments are *mysteries* of faith, like the Holy Trinity or the Incarnation. We accept and firmly believe in them because God has revealed them to us. One of the most ancient titles for the sacraments (still used in the prayers at Mass) is **sacred mysteries**.

When a priest performs the sign of a sacrament, the message he proclaims is also carried out. For example, when the priest says, "This is my Body. . . . This is the cup of my Blood . . . ." over the bread and wine at Mass, they really do become the Body and Blood of the Lord, because Jesus gave him the power to do this. Every sacrament works *ex opere operato*, which means "from the work accomplished." Jesus has already accomplished the work of salvation that gives power to every sacrament

today. The power of God is actively present every time a sacrament is celebrated in accordance with the Church's intention, regardless of the minister's own virtue or holiness.

The sacraments are not just signs, but *efficacious* signs. They *confer* the grace that they signify: Christ himself communicates the grace that is signified by the sacrament (CCC 1127). At the same time, we should understand that "the fruits of the sacraments also depend on the disposition of the one who receives them" (CCC 1128). It is necessary for us to make room in our hearts and be ready for what God intends to give us in the sacraments.

Here is a list that will help you learn the matter and form of the sacraments.

BAPTISM: The pouring of water while saying: "I baptize you in the Name of the Father, and of the Son, and of the Holy Spirit."
CONFIRMATION: The bishop's imposing his

hand on the person and anointing him with chrism (blessed oil) while these words are said: "Be sealed with the Gift of the Holy Spirit."

HOLY EUCHARIST: The gifts of bread and wine over which the priest says: "This is my Body. . . . This is the cup of my Blood. . . ."

PENANCE: The verbal confession of sins to a priest, after which he says: "I absolve you from your sins in the name of the Father, and of the Son, and of the Holy Spirit. *Amen.*"

ANOINTING: Anointing with oil of the sick while saying: "Through this holy anointing may the Lord in his love and mercy help you with the grace of the Holy Spirit. *Amen.* May the Lord, who frees you from sin, save you and raise you up. *Amen.*"

HOLY ORDERS: The bishop's laying on of hands followed by his saying "We ask you, all-powerful Father, give these servants of yours the dignity of the presbyterate. Renew the Spirit of holiness within them. By your divine gift may they attain the second order in the hierarchy and exemplify right conduct in their lives."

MATRIMONY: The exchange of wedding vows between a Christian man and a Christian woman.

The Gift of Sacramental Grace

Besides giving us sanctifying grace the sacraments give us a special grace for our journey to heaven. It is called **sacramental grace**, and it helps us in various ways, depending upon from which sacrament it comes. The following list shows us these different sacramental graces:

BAPTISM: Gives us the grace to live a holy life.

CONFIRMATION: Gives us the grace to be strong in faith and loyal to Jesus as we journey to heaven.

HOLY EUCHARIST: Gives us the grace to love Jesus with all our hearts and to love our neighbors as ourselves.

PENANCE: Gives us the grace to overcome our sinful desires and actions.

ANOINTING: Gives us the grace to accept our sicknesses and to die a good death.

HOLY ORDERS: Gives priests the grace to live good lives dedicated to preaching the Gospel and administering the sacraments.

MATRIMONY: Gives a husband and a wife the grace of loving each other until death and of being good parents.

Words to Know:

sacrament   sign
sacred mysteries   sacramental grace

Q. 119 *What are the sacraments?*
The sacraments are visible signs instituted by Jesus Christ to give us grace and to make us holy (CCC 1131).

Q. 120 *What are the seven sacraments?*
The seven sacraments are Baptism, Confirmation, Holy Eucharist, Penance, Anointing of the Sick, Holy Orders, and Matrimony (CCC 1113).

Q. 121 *Who gave the sacraments the power of conferring grace?*

Jesus Christ gave the sacraments the power of conferring grace which he merited for us by his Passion, death, and Resurrection (CCC 1115, 1127).

Q. 122 *What kinds of graces do we obtain through the sacraments?*

Through the sacraments we obtain sanctifying grace and sacramental grace (CCC 1129).

Q. 123 *What is sacramental grace?*

Sacramental grace is the grace of the Holy Spirit given by Jesus Christ that is proper to each of the sacraments (CCC 1129, 2003).

Q. 124 *How do sacraments make us holy?*

The sacraments make us holy either by giving us sanctifying grace or restoring it, or by increasing the grace which we already possess (CCC 1127, 1129).

Q. 125 *Which sacraments give us the grace of justification, or sanctifying grace?*

The grace of justification, or sanctifying grace, is given to us at Baptism and Penance, which are sometimes called "sacraments of the dead" because they give life to souls that have been dead through sin (CCC 1279, 1446).

Q. 126 *Which sacraments increase grace in us?*

The sacraments that increase grace in us are Confirmation, the Eucharist, the Anointing of the Sick, Holy Orders, and Matrimony (CCC 1131).

Q. 127 *How do we grow in the grace of the sacraments?*

We grow in the grace of sacraments by receiving them with the proper disposition and living according to Jesus' teaching (CCC 1128).

Q. 128 *What three things are required for a sacrament?*

The three things required for a sacrament are the matter, the form, and the minister of the sacrament (CCC 1812–13).

Q. 129 *What is the matter of sacrament?*

The matter of sacrament is the things or actions of which it is composed, such as water in baptism (CCC 1084).

Q. 130 *What is the form of a sacrament?*

The form of a sacrament is the set of words pronounced by the minister in administering the sacrament (CCC 1084).

Q. 131 *Who is the minister of a sacrament?*

The minister of a sacrament is the person who has the power to confer the sacrament in the Name of Jesus Christ (CCC 1084).

CHAPTER 17

God Calls Us To Reconciliation

"Truly, truly, I say to you, unless one is born of water and the Spirit, he cannot enter the kingdom of God."

John 3:5

In his letter to the Christians in Rome, the Apostle Paul tells us that the entire human race was separated from God because of the original sin of Adam. But he goes on to write that this separation has been brought to an end by Jesus our Savior:

> But God shows his love for us in that while we were yet sinners Christ died for us. Since, therefore, we are now justified by his blood, much more shall we be saved by him from the wrath of God. For if while we were enemies we were reconciled to God by the death of his Son, much more, now that we are reconciled, shall we be saved by his life (Rom 5:8–10).

This **reconciliation**, or reunion, of mankind with God in loving friendship, is called the *good news* of our salvation. Even though mankind had turned away from God by disobedience, he continued to love us and wanted us to be reunited with him. His love was so great that he sent his only Son to earth in order to offer us forgiveness and new life, to call each one of us to reconciliation: "For God so loved the world that he gave his only Son, that

whoever believes in him should not perish but have eternal life" (Jn 3:16).

God Calls Us through His Church

God's call to reconciliation comes to us through the Catholic Church which Jesus founded to be his voice in the world. Through the Church God invites us to answer his call by receiving the Sacrament of Baptism. At Baptism we are freed from the separation caused by original sin and are brought back into friendship with God through his grace.

When adults ask for Baptism they are aware of God's call. Most of us were baptized as infants, however; our parents answered God's call for us. Now we are old enough to answer for ourselves. We can understand that God has asked us to receive his friendship through Christ and the Church. The ordinary minister of Baptism is one who has received the Sacrament of Holy Orders. However, in cases of emergency, anyone can baptize using the proper matter (water) and form (the words, "I baptize you in the Name of the Father, and of the Son, and of the Holy Spirit.").

Jesus Gave Us Baptism

One night a man named Nicodemus came to talk with Jesus. He was a secret follower of Our Lord who wanted to know more about Christ's teachings. During their conversation Jesus told Nicodemus that Baptism was necessary for those who wanted to go to heaven, saying: "Truly, truly, I say to you, unless one is born of water and the Spirit, he cannot enter the kingdom of God" (Jn 3:5).

In order to make this spiritual rebirth possible, Jesus gave us the sacrament of Baptism. After his Resurrection he said to the apostles:

Go therefore and make disciples of all nations, baptizing them in the name of the Father and of the Son and of the Holy Spirit (Mt 28:19).

After receiving the Holy Spirit the apostles preached the importance of Baptism to the people in Jerusalem. On that very first Pentecost Sunday, Saint Peter proclaimed to the crowds:

Repent, and be baptized every one of you in the name of Jesus Christ for the forgiveness of your sins; and you shall receive the gift of the Holy Spirit (Acts 2:38).

Through the preaching of the apostles, thousands of people responded to God's call to reconciliation and received the Sacrament of Baptism. Men, women, and children from every nation were united with God and became members of his Holy Church.

The Effects of Baptism

Baptism is the first sacrament we receive. It can be received only once because it gives us a special unrepeatable sign called the **Baptismal seal**. This invisible mark shows God that we have been united to Jesus by Baptism and have become his adopted children. It can never be taken away, not even by mortal sin. We also receive Baptism first, because it gives us the right to receive the other sacraments.

Although Jesus did not need Baptism, because he was without sin, we can learn what this sacrament does for *us* by looking at his baptism in the River Jordan. This baptism that Saint John the Baptist gave was a way of helping others to show their sorrow for sin.

The word "baptism" means "washing." This reminds us that through Baptism, God washes away original sin from our souls. If the person being baptized is old enough to have sinned himself, it also takes these offenses away and also their temporal punishment for those sins.

When Our Lord came up out of the water, the Holy Spirit descended upon him in the form of a dove. The Holy Spirit comes down upon us, too, and fills us with the new life of sanctifying grace. We become his holy temples

93

just as the Apostle Paul said in his first letter to the Corinthians: "Do you not know that your body is a temple of the Holy Spirit within you, which you have from God?" (1 Cor 6:19).

When the Spirit came down upon Jesus the people heard the voice of God the Father saying: "This is my beloved Son, with whom I am well pleased" (Mt 3:17).

At our Baptism we become the beloved children of the Father. Sanctifying grace gives us this precious gift. And since we are his children, we also receive the right to live in our Father's heavenly Kingdom. He gives us the supernatural powers of faith, hope, and charity that help us live lives worthy of this Kingdom.

Baptism of Desire and of Blood

You might wonder what happens to those people who have not received Baptism. Do they go to heaven, too? There are two other ways of getting to heaven for those who do not know about the sacrament or who have not been able to receive it before they die.

One of these ways is called **Baptism of desire**. This means that those who are sorry for their sins and who cooperate with God's grace by trying to please him as best they know how can be saved too. Perhaps these people cannot receive Baptism because there is no one to give it to them; or maybe they are planning to be baptized but die before receiving it. Baptism of desire can also save those who are truly ignorant of the sacrament, but who would receive it if they knew that it was necessary for salvation.

The other way of getting to heaven is called **Baptism of blood**. It has happened many times when a non-Christian gives up his life in martyrdom for Jesus. Quite often, during times when Catholics were persecuted for the faith, many non-believers would be so moved by the martyrs' heroism that they would defend the believers and join them in martyrdom. Thus, even though they had not received the sacrament, they showed faith in Jesus and were saved.

As mentioned earlier, Baptism enables us to receive the other sacraments. In fact, it becomes one of the duties of the baptized: to live a sacramental life (to receive the sacraments), obey the Church's teachings, read Scripture, learn about the Catholic Faith, attend Mass, and lead a life of prayer. God will give us the sacramental grace of Baptism we need to fulfill our duties.

Words to Know:

reconciliation   Baptismal seal
Baptism of desire   Baptism of blood

Q. 132 *What is Baptism?*

Baptism is the sacrament that makes us Christians, that is, followers of Jesus Christ, sons of God, and members of the Church (CCC 1213).

Q. 133 *What is the matter of Baptism?*

The matter of Baptism is water (CCC 1228, 1239).

Q. 134 *What is the form of Baptism?*

The form of Baptism is the following words: "I baptize you in the Name of the Father, and of the Son, and of the Holy Spirit." (CCC 1240).

Q. 135 *Who is the minister of Baptism?*

The ordinary minister of Baptism is one who has received Holy Orders but, in case of necessity, anyone can baptize provided he has the intention of doing what the Church does (CCC 1256).

Q. 136 *How is Baptism given?*

Baptism is given by immersing a person in water or pouring water on his head three times while saying "I baptize you in the Name of the Father, and of the Son, and of the Holy Spirit" (CCC 1239–40).

Q. 137 *What effects does Baptism produce?*

Baptism makes the baptized person a child of God and a member of the Church by removing original sin and any personal sin, bestowing the life of grace, marking the baptized person as belonging to Christ, and enabling him to receive the other sacraments (CCC 1279–80).

Q. 138 *Why can Baptism be received only once?*

Baptism can be received only once because it impresses a permanent spiritual mark, or character, on the soul, which distinguishes a person as Christ's own forever (CCC 1246, 1274, 1280).

Q. 139 *If Baptism is necessary for all men, is no one saved without Baptism?*

Without Baptism, no one can be saved. However, when it is impossible to receive the Sacrament of Baptism, the Baptism of blood, which is martyrdom for Jesus Christ or Baptism of desire, desire for Baptism, brings about the benefits of the Sacrament of Baptism (CCC 1257–60).

Q. 140 *What are the duties of one who is baptized?*

One who is baptized has the duties of following the teachings of Jesus Christ as found in his Church, including believing the faith of the Church, receiving the sacraments, and obeying the Church's pastors (CCC 1273).

CHAPTER 18

The Rite of Baptism

"Go therefore and make disciples of all nations, baptizing them in the name of the Father and of the Son and of the Holy Spirit, teaching them to observe all that I have commanded you; and lo, I am with you always, to the close of the age."

Matthew 28:19–20

We know that Jesus instituted, or gave us, the Sacrament of Baptism and that he told his followers to give it to others by using water and calling upon the Name of the Holy Trinity. In this chapter we will learn why water is used in this sacrament and how the rite (ceremony) is carried out today.

The Use of Water

Christ chose water as the **sign of Baptism** because it had deep meaning to God's people. They knew, from the book of Genesis, that the Spirit began the work of creation in the waters of the world (Gen 1:2). They also remembered that God had used water to destroy all evil men in Noah's time and that Noah and his family were saved by passing through the waters of the flood. In their own history of salvation the Jews recalled how God had used the waters of the Red Sea to save his people and how the waves parted for them to pass through. The Jews also crossed the waters of the Jordan to enter into the Promised Land. In all these events the people had come to see that God had used water both as a way of destroying evil and of doing good for them.

Through the work of Saint John the Baptist they also saw water as a way of showing the desire to be cleansed of sin since they had repented. So it was quite easy for them to accept it as God's sign of actually taking sin away.

But ordinary water by itself cannot free us from sin or give us the new life of grace. Only when it is used in Baptism according to the plan of Jesus can it do this. This means that the water must be poured over the head of the person to be baptized while the priest says these words: "I baptize you in the Name of the Father, and of the Son, and of the Holy Spirit."

These words tell us that the person is being *consecrated* to the Holy Trinity. He is being made a child of the Father; a brother or sister of Jesus Christ; and a temple of the Holy Spirit.

The Rite of Baptism

We will learn much about the sacrament by taking a look at the full **rite** (ceremony) of

Baptism of infants that is used by the Catholic Church today.

First, the infant to be baptized is brought to the church by his parents and godparents. Godparents have the duty of assisting the parents in raising the children in the Catholic Faith. The priest, who represents Jesus for us, meets the family at the entrance and welcomes the baby into the community of God. This shows us that by Baptism we are made members of the holy Church.

Then the Liturgy of the Word takes place. The readings remind us that God has commanded Baptism for our salvation. After the

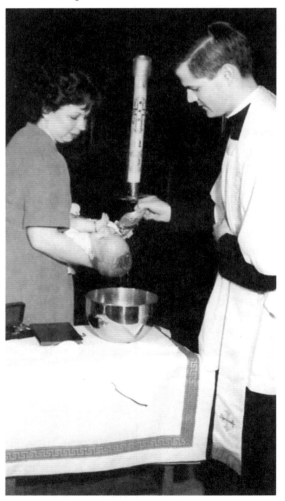

homily and *Litany of the Saints* (after one of whom we are usually named), the ceremony reaches its most important part: the exorcism and actual Baptism with water.

We know that original sin put us under the evil influence of the devil, for Adam and Eve chose to believe him rather than God. **Exorcism** is the Church's powerful way of destroying this influence. The prayer of exorcism says:

Almighty and ever-living God, you sent your only Son into the world to cast out the power of Satan, spirit of evil, to rescue man from the kingdom of darkness, and bring him into the splendor of your Kingdom of light. We pray for this child: set him free from original sin, make him a temple of your glory, and send your Holy Spirit to dwell within him. We ask this through Christ Our Lord. *Amen* (Rite of Baptism).

After the exorcism the priest anoints the baby with the **oil of the catechumens**. Next, the baby, through the lips of his parents and godparents, rejects sin and satan and accepts the teachings of Jesus as stated in the Creed. Then the priest carries out the actual sacrament by pouring water while saying the words of Baptism. The final ceremonial actions are the anointing with chrism, the clothing, and the lighting of the baptismal candle.

The anointing is done with a special oil called **sacred chrism**. This is consecrated by the bishop and is used to show that the new Christian shares in Christ's triple office as priest, prophet, and king. The priest says this prayer while anointing the baby:

God the Father of Our Lord Jesus Christ has freed you from sin, given you a new birth by water and the Holy Spirit, and welcomed you into his holy People. He now anoints you with the chrism of salvation. As Christ was anointed Priest, Prophet, and King, so may you live always as members of his body, sharing everlasting life. *Amen* (Rite of Baptism).

Then the infant receives a white garment. The color white is an ancient symbol for purity and sinlessness. A new white candle is also given to him as a reminder of Our Lord, who is the true Light of the world (Jn 9:5). It also calls to mind Jesus' words to his followers: "You are the light of the world. . . . Let your light so shine before men, that they may see your good works and give glory to your Father who is in heaven" (Mt 5:14–16).

Living Our Baptismal Commitment

At Baptism we make a **vow**, or solemn promise to God. We vow to give up sin and live according to the teachings of Christ. In order to keep this promise we need to pray and receive the sacraments of Penance and Holy Eucharist often.

We must also study the Catholic faith. This is why your religion class is very important for you. It helps you to live in faith, hope, and charity as you journey toward heaven, your eternal home.

Words to Know:
sign of Baptism   rite   exorcism
sacred chrism   oil of the catechumens   vow

Q. 141 *What does one renounce when receiving Baptism?*
When receiving Baptism, one renounces satan and sin (CCC 1237).

Q. 142 *How do infants renounce the devil in their Baptism?*
Infants renounce the devil in their Baptism by means of their godparents (CCC 1231).

Q. 143 *Who are godparents in Baptism?*
The godparents become spiritual parents who assume responsibility for the Christian education of their godchild if the parents should fail in the matter; hence the godparents should be good Christians (CCC 1253, 1255).

Q. 144 *What does sacred chrism signify?*
Sacred chrism signifies the gift of the Holy Spirit and the baptized person's incorporation into Christ who is anointed priest, prophet, and king (CCC 1241).

Q. 145 *What does the white garment signify?*

The white garment signifies that we put on a new identity in Christ, one that is pure and radiant in his grace (CCC 1243).

Q. 146 *What does the baptismal candle signify?*

The baptismal candle signifies our receiving Christ who is the Light of the world into our lives and his grace into our souls (CCC 1243).

Q. 147 *What is an exorcism?*

An exorcism is the casting out by the Church in the Name of Jesus of any evil spirit or evil oppression from the soul (CCC 1673).

CHAPTER 19

The Sacrament of Confirmation

Now when the apostles at Jerusalem heard that Samaria had received the word of God, they sent to them Peter and John, who came down and prayed for them that they might receive the Holy Spirit; for it had not yet fallen on any of them, but they had only been baptized in the name of the Lord Jesus. Then they laid their hands on them and they received the Holy Spirit.

Acts 8:14–17

During the Last Supper the apostles knew that Jesus was saying farewell to them. He was talking about going to someplace where they could not yet follow (Jn 13:36). Jesus knew that this saddened them, so he promised to send Someone who would give them comfort and strengthen their faith:

And I will pray the Father, and he will give you another Counselor, to be with you for ever, even the Spirit of truth, whom the world cannot receive, because it neither sees him nor knows him; you know him, for he dwells with you, and will be in you (Jn 14:16–17).

The word **Paraclete** means counselor, someone who helps and guides others, an advocate. The "Spirit of Truth," who is the Third Person of the Holy Trinity, was to come to the followers of Jesus as a counselor to give inner strength and help their friendship with Jesus to remain alive and active. He would give them all the spiritual help they needed in order to spread the faith among others.

The Promise Fulfilled

After Jesus returned to the Father, the apostles and other disciples of Jesus spent nine days with Mary, the Mother of Jesus, in prayer, asking God to send the gift of the Holy Spirit. On Pentecost Sunday the promise was fulfilled as Saint Luke tells us:

When the day of Pentecost had come, they were all together in one place. And suddenly a sound came from heaven like the rush of a mighty wind, and it filled all the house where they were sitting. And there appeared to them tongues as of fire, distributed and resting on each one of them. And they were all filled with the Holy Spirit and began to speak in

> But the Counselor, the Holy Spirit, whom the Father will send in my name, he will teach you all things, and bring to your remembrance all that I have said to you.
>
> (John 14:26)

other tongues, as the Spirit gave them utterance (Acts 2:1–4).

The unusual symbols of wind and fire reveal the powers which the Spirit gives us. Wind is an invisible but very real force: it can even lift houses and cars off the ground! Fire is something that cleanses things; for example, sometimes fire is used to clear a piece of land of shrubs and other rubbish so that new trees can be planted. So the Spirit is like an invisi-

ble power within us that cleanses our hearts of sin and selfish desires. In other words, he makes us strong and mature Christians.

We Receive the Fullness of the Spirit

While it is Baptism that first gives us the Holy Spirit, *Confirmation* increases his power within us. This sacrament strengthens the new life we have received as infants. It helps us to **witness** or stand up for Jesus among our friends and classmates.

The New Testament does not tell us just when Our Lord gave this sacrament to the Church, but the day of Pentecost is usually seen as the first "Confirmation," and throughout the Acts of the Apostles we see many instances of the apostles confirming new believers. When the followers of Jesus baptized people, they would send for one of the apostles to come and give Confirmation to the new Christians. Usually the bishop is the minister of this sacrament, although he may delegate this faculty to priests.

The **sign of Confirmation** is the laying on of hands and the anointing with sacred chrism. The laying on of hands shows us that a spiritual gift is being handed on to the Christian; the chrism reminds us of our share in Jesus' triple office and connects this sacrament with Baptism. The words which the bishop says (". . . be sealed with the Gift of the Holy Spirit") tell us what gift is being handed on.

The Effects of Confirmation

Like Baptism, Confirmation gives us a seal, or spiritual mark, that shows we are Christians. It deepens the life of sanctifying grace and increases it within us. While at Baptism we were spiritual infants, now we are made spiritual adults who are given the responsibility of spreading the faith to others. This is the special meaning and commitment of Confirmation.

In order to spread the faith the Spirit gives us special gifts which we will learn about in the next chapter. Like the twelve apostles we can be truly transformed into courageous followers of the Lord, who are willing even to lay down our lives for the love of God and the truths of the faith.

The Rite of Confirmation

This beautiful sacrament usually takes place during a special "Mass of the Holy Spirit" that is celebrated by a bishop. It is like other Masses except that the prayers and readings are all about the role of the Holy Spirit in the life of the Catholic Christian. The administration of the Sacrament of Confirmation takes place after the homily.

First, since Confirmation is a strengthening of Baptism, the bishop leads everyone in the renewal of the baptismal vows. Once again we reject sin and satan; we profess the Creed and profess our loyalty to Jesus. Then the bishop stretches out his hands over the group to be confirmed while praying:

All-powerful God, Father of Our Lord Jesus Christ, by water and the Holy Spirit you freed your sons and daughters from sin and gave them new life. Send your Holy Spirit upon them to be their Helper and Guide. Give them the spirit of wisdom and understanding, the spirit of right judgment and courage, the spirit of knowledge and reverence. Fill them with the spirit of wonder and awe in your presence. We ask this through Christ Our Lord. *Amen* (Rite of Confirmation).

After this comes the actual administration of the sacrament through the anointing with sacred chrism and the laying on of hands. Each candidate, together with his sponsor, comes before the bishop. The bishop dips his right thumb into the chrism and places his hand on the head of the person being confirmed, making the Sign of the Cross with the chrism on the forehead of the candidate, while saying:

(Confirmation Name), be sealed with the Gift of the Holy Spirit.

The newly confirmed answers, "Amen." The bishop then says, "Peace be with you," and the newly confirmed answers, "And also with you." Through this sacred rite the person has been sealed with the Spirit and has received the outpouring of his powerful gifts, which he received at Baptism. (Of course, to receive this gift most fruitfully, we must come to our Confirmation in the state of grace and with a spirit of faith in God.) The Mass then continues as usual, and at the end a special blessing is given to the newly confirmed Catholics.

Living as Mature Christians

The closing prayer for the Mass of the Holy Spirit reveals how we are to live as mature followers of Jesus:

God our Father, complete the work you have begun and keep the gifts of your Holy Spirit active in the hearts of your people. Make them ready to *live his gospel* and eager to *do his will.* May they *never be ashamed to proclaim to all the world Christ crucified,* living and reigning for ever and ever. *Amen* (Rite of Confirmation).

This is a very big mission for the new adult Christians! But the Holy Spirit helps us to carry it out. One way he does this is by giving us the good examples of the saints. They show us that everyone, no matter what age or situation in life, can live the gospel, do God's will, and proclaim Jesus to others. This is the main reason why we receive Baptismal, and sometimes

Confirmation, names. We are placed under the spiritual protection of one of God's saints to whom we pray and who prays for us and inspires us by the example of his or her life. This holy person becomes our **patron saint**.

Q. 148 *What is the Sacrament of Confirmation?*

The Sacrament of Confirmation makes us more perfect Christians and soldiers of Christ by means of the outpouring of the Holy Spirit and the strengthening of his gifts which we first received at Baptism (CCC 1285, 1316).

Q. 149 *What is the matter of Confirmation?*

The matter of Confirmation is the anointing with sacred chrism (CCC 1293, 1300).

Q. 150 *What is the form of Confirmation?*

The form of Confirmation is the following words: "Be sealed with the Gift of the Holy Spirit" (CCC 1300).

Q. 151 *Who is the minister of Confirmation?*

The ordinary minister of Confirmation is a bishop, although a priest may receive special facilities to administer the Sacrament of Confirmation (CCC 1313).

Q. 152 *How does the bishop administer Confirmation?*

The bishop administers Confirmation to the one being confirmed by anointing him with chrism on the forehead, which is done by the laying on of the hand, and through the words, "Be sealed with the gift of the Holy Spirit" (CCC 1300).

Q. 153 *How does Confirmation make us more perfect Christians?*

Confirmation makes us more perfect Christians and witnesses of Jesus Christ by giving us an abundance of the Holy Spirit, his grace and his gifts, which confirm and strengthen us in faith and in the other virtues (CCC 1303).

Q. 154 *What does the anointing on the forehead in the form of a cross signify?*

The anointing on the forehead in the form of a cross signifies that the confirmed person, as a brave witness of Jesus Christ, should not be ashamed of the Cross nor fear enemies of the faith (CCC 1295–96).

Q. 155 *Who are the sponsors in Confirmation?*

The sponsors should be good Christians in order to give good example and spiritual assistance to those who are confirmed (CCC 1311).

Q. 156 *What are the duties of one who is confirmed?*

One who is confirmed has the duties of witnessing to and defending the Faith, and continuing to live his baptismal promises.

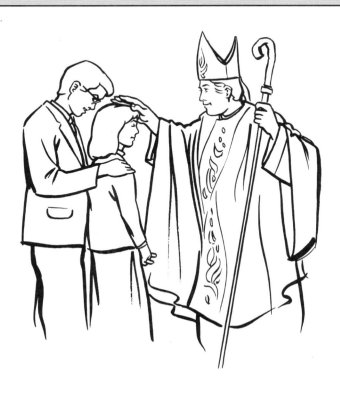

CHAPTER 20

The Gifts of the Holy Spirit

You will know them by their fruits. Are grapes gathered from thorns, or figs from thistles?

Matthew 7:16

At the Last Supper Jesus spoke about a very special gift that he was going to give his followers: "If a man loves me, he will keep my word, and my Father will love him, and we will come to him and make our home with him" (Jn 14:23).

Jesus tells us that God will actually come to live within those who love him and obey his commands! And where the Father and Son are, of course, the Spirit will be there also. This gift of God-within-us is called the **indwelling** of the Trinity. As long as we are in the state of sanctifying grace, God will live in our souls. Saint Paul wrote about this in his first letter to the Corinthians: "Do you not know that you are God's temple and that God's Spirit dwells in you? If any one destroys God's temple, God will destroy him. For God's temple is holy, and that temple you are" (1 Cor 3:16–17).

The mystery of God-within-us is often mentioned in the New Testament by Saint Paul. He reminds us that this presence makes us more than God's creatures—it makes us his children: "And because you are sons, God has sent the Spirit of his Son into our hearts, crying, 'Abba! Father!' " (Gal 4:6).

The Gifts of the Holy Spirit

Along with this holy presence of God, the Spirit brings *seven gifts* to our souls at Baptism. We receive an outpouring of these **seven gifts of the Holy Spirit** at Confirmation. They are the same spiritual powers that were poured out upon Jesus as he began his mission of preaching the good news of salvation. The prophet Isaiah foretold these gifts eight hundred years before Jesus was born:

And the Spirit of the LORD shall rest upon him, the spirit of wisdom and understanding, the spirit of counsel and might, the spirit of knowledge and the fear of the LORD. And his delight shall be in the fear of the LORD (Is 11:2–3).

Let us look carefully at each of these important gifts, to learn what they are meant to do for our lives:

WISDOM: Helps us to see that the world is only a temporary place for us, that heaven is our true home. It helps us to set our hearts on the things that really count in life, such as

God, virtue, and prayer. It helps us to see things as God sees them.

UNDERSTANDING: Gives us an insight into the mysteries of faith and helps us to explain the faith to others.

KNOWLEDGE: Helps us to see everything in life in relation to God and eternity, to know him, the world he created, and his plan for men.

COUNSEL: Helps us to make correct decisions about God's will for our lives.

FORTITUDE: Gives us the strength to be faithful to Christ even when it is difficult to do so.

PIETY: Inspires us to worship God and to love him as our Father and to love our neighbor as our self.

FEAR OF THE LORD: Shows us the evil of sin and helps us to desire to live in God's grace. It is also called "wonder and awe" in God's presence because it reminds us that he is great and all-powerful.

Many people wonder if they really have these gifts; they don't seem to be present in their lives. Perhaps these Christians have looked upon the gifts as some kind of magic—they expect them to "pop up" when needed. But this is not how the gifts work in us. Like faith, hope, and charity, we have to exercise our spiritual muscles in order to use these wonderful powers. We must pray to the Holy Spirit asking him to show us how to use them. Try to memorize these gifts and then ask God to help you use them when a need arises. For example, if you are strongly tempted to go to a party where drugs or alcohol will be used, ask for the gift of fortitude to help you overcome the temptation. The Holy Spirit *will* answer your prayer and show you what to do.

The Fruits of the Holy Spirit

As we grow in prayer and in the use of these seven gifts, we will see certain effects taking place in our lives. These are called the **twelve fruits of the Holy Spirit**. When we see a tree that is blossoming and producing delicious fruit, we know that it is a healthy plant. It is the same with the Christian life. We will know that our spiritual life is healthy if we see these fruits in our relationships with God and others.

The twelve fruits of the Spirit are:

1. CHARITY: Love for God and for others.

2. JOY: Happiness in living the Christian life.

3. PEACE: Inner calmness, even in difficulties.

4. PATIENCE: Kindly putting up with the faults of others.

5. KINDNESS: Sympathy and concern for the needs of others.

6. GOODNESS: Giving good example in all that we do.

7. GENEROSITY: Willingness to share our time and possessions with those in need.

8. GENTLENESS: Being gentle in our words and deeds toward others.

9. FAITHFULNESS: Loyalty to God and the people we are committed to, such as one's parents, spouse, and good friends.

10. MODESTY: Respecting ourselves and others in conversations, dress, etc.

11. SELF-CONTROL: Proper balance in our desire for pleasure.

12. CHASTITY: Proper attitude toward others and control over our sexual desires.

Jesus told us that we will produce these fruits of the Spirit only if we are united with him through prayer and the sacraments. He compared himself to a vine which carries sap to its branches; the "sap" is a symbol for his grace and power: "I am the vine, you are the branches. He who abides in me, and I in him, he it is that bears much fruit, for apart from me you can do nothing" (Jn 15:5).

Words to Know:
indwelling   seven gifts of the Holy Spirit
twelve fruits of the Holy Spirit

Q. 157 *What are the seven gifts of the Holy Spirit?*
The seven gifts of the Holy Spirit are wisdom, understanding, counsel, fortitude, knowledge, piety, and fear of the Lord (CCC 1831).

Q. 158 *What are the twelve fruits of the Holy Spirit?*
The twelve fruits of the Holy Spirit are charity, joy, peace, patience, kindness, goodness, generosity, gentleness, faithfulness, modesty, self-control, and chastity (CCC 1832).

CHAPTER 21

The Sacrament of the Holy Eucharist

For as often as you eat this bread and drink the cup, you proclaim the Lord's death until he comes.

1 Corinthians 11:26

One day during his public ministry, Jesus found himself in the midst of more than five thousand people. They had all come to hear him preach about the good news of salvation. Before they knew it, it was dinnertime, and the people were extremely hungry. Jesus looked with love upon them and said to his apostles, "How are we to buy bread, so that these people may eat?" (Jn 6:5).

Now Jesus knew exactly what he was going to do, but he wanted to test his friends' faith in him. Philip reminded Jesus that it would cost over half a year's wages to feed such a crowd. Andrew brought the Lord five loaves of bread and a couple of fish, but wondered what good they would be for so many. Jesus blessed these small portions and told the apostles to hand them out to the crowd. A miracle! There was more than enough food, with twelve full baskets left over!

Jesus, the Bread of Life

The people were amazed and wanted Jesus to do this again. Why not send bread (manna) down from heaven just as God did for our people during the Exodus? they asked. Jesus revealed to them that God was going to give his people a much greater bread; he was telling them about the Holy Eucharist:

"I am the bread of life. Your fathers ate the manna in the wilderness, and they died. This is the bread which comes down from heaven, that a man may eat of it and not die. I am the living bread which came down from heaven; if any one eats of this bread, he will live for ever; and the bread which I shall give for the life of the world is my flesh." The Jews then disputed among themselves, saying, "How can this man give us his flesh to eat?" So Jesus said to them, "Truly, truly, I say to you, unless you eat the flesh of the Son of man and drink his blood, you have no life in you; he who eats my flesh and drinks my blood has eternal life, and I will raise him up at the last day" (Jn 6:48–54).

The listeners were horrified! Eat his flesh and drink his blood! Does he think we are cannibals? they wondered. Even having seen this great miracle, they did not trust Jesus enough to know that he would not ask such a thing. He was going to change bread and wine into his Flesh and Blood. It would still taste like ordinary food, but it would *really* be Jesus himself. Many disciples left Our Lord that day, but the twelve apostles remained firm in their faith. They awaited the day when he would give them this holy bread of life.

Jesus Gives Us the Holy Eucharist

At the Last Supper, Jesus kept his promise and gave God's people the bread of eternal life. The evangelist Saint Matthew, who was an eyewitness of this event, tells us about it in his Gospel:

Now as they were eating, Jesus took bread, and blessed, and broke it, and gave it to the disciples and said, "Take, eat; this is my body." And he took a cup, and when he had given thanks he gave it to them, saying, "Drink of it, all of you; for this is my blood of the covenant, which is poured out for many for the forgiveness of sins" (Mt 26:26–28).

Just as he had changed water into wine at the beginning of his ministry, so now he was changing bread and wine into his very Body and Blood. This was the first Holy Mass, or *Eucharist* as we often call it today. The word "eucharist" is from the Greek word for "thanksgiving," and it is used as a name for the Mass because Jesus gave thanks to the Father while

consecrating the bread and wine. There are many other names by which this holy Sacrament is known: Lord's Supper, Blessed Sacrament, Sacrament of the Altar, Bread of Life, Holy Communion, and Holy Sacrifice of the Mass.

The Sign of the Sacrament

We can learn the most obvious purpose of the Eucharist by looking at the **sign of the Holy Eucharist**: bread and wine, together with the words of Consecration ("This is my Body. . . . This is the cup of my Blood. . . ."). They tell us that food is being given to us, but it is supernatural food—the Flesh and Blood of the Son of God!

These two sources of nourishment, bread and wine, were an important part of the diet of the people of the Holy Land. Bread was their main food and wine was the most common beverage. To them these two items meant life and health for the body; Jesus made them the life and health of the soul as well. Without the Holy Eucharist our souls would starve to death!

Today, with so many different kinds of foods available to us, we do not see the importance of bread and wine as clearly as our ancestors did. But if you think about it, you will realize that so many of our favorite foods are made out of wheat flour, "which earth has given and human hands have made" (Offertory prayer over the bread). And even to this day wine is used as *the* celebration drink at weddings, parties, and many other get-togethers.

The Mystery of the Eucharist

At the Consecration of the Mass, the priest changes the bread and the wine by the power which he received at ordination. This change is known as **transubstantiation**. If we break this word apart we can see what it is trying to express. *Trans* here means "change" and *substantiation* comes from "substance" or what a thing is. At Mass the "things" are bread and wine, so the word is simply saying that these things change into Jesus Christ.

Our Lord chose appropriate means by which we could receive this Sacrament: he gave it to us under the *appearances* of bread and wine. When we go to Holy Communion we see and taste ordinary food, but our faith in Jesus tells us that it is not what it seems. We are really eating the Flesh of the Son of Man and drinking his Blood.

This is why the Eucharist is called the **Mystery of Faith**. We can only accept it on God's word. At every Mass, right after the Consecration, the priest says to us, "Let us proclaim the Mystery of Faith." He invites us to recite a prayer of faith in the **Real Presence** of Jesus in this sacrament.

The bread and wine are not changed into Jesus' Flesh and Blood just for a time during Mass. They remain the Body and Blood of the Lord after Mass, and the Host is reverently kept in the **tabernacle** in the church. This is a special, solid, immovable container that is decorated with symbols of Jesus. A vigil lamp (candle) is kept burning before the tabernacle day and night as a way of honoring Jesus in the Eucharist.

Saint Cyril of Jerusalem (d. 386) was a holy bishop and doctor (exceptionally great teacher) of the Church. He used to encourage the Catholics in his diocese to have faith in the Real Presence saying:

When Christ says, "This is my Body," who should dare to doubt him? When he says, "This is my Blood," who dares to say that it is not? Once he changed water into wine. Does he not deserve our faith in being able to change wine into his Blood? Do not think of the Blessed Sacrament as ordinary bread, for according to the words of Christ, it is his Flesh. Even though your senses do not convince you, let your faith strengthen you that you do not judge according to your taste (*Catecheses mystagogicae*, 4).

The Effects of the Holy Eucharist

When we receive the Blessed Sacrament worthily—that is, free from mortal sin, having fasted from food and drink (except water and medicine) for one hour beforehand, and approaching the altar with faith—Jesus does wonderful things for our souls!

He increases the life of grace within us and takes away our venial sins. He actually makes us one with him. He is truly within us after Holy Communion.

He unites us with one another, for we all are made one with the same Eucharistic Lord. Holy Communion helps us to love one another.

He helps us to overcome our faults and sinful desires. By the frequent reception of the Eucharist we are given the power to give up all our sins and even our selfish desires.

With each Holy Communion Christ's life increases in us. Those who receive the Eucharist often and worthily will have a deeper relationship with Jesus in heaven.

Lastly, Our Lord prepares us for the resurrection of the dead. The Creed tells us that everyone will rise from the dead at the end of the world. Those who go often to Communion with faith, hope, and love will be more sure of being in heaven, body and soul, someday.

But if we do not receive him *properly*, we will not profit from this Sacrament. As a matter of fact, to receive Communion with a mortal sin is one of the worst offenses against the Lord. It is called a **sacrilege** and must be confessed as soon as possible.

Words to Know:

sign of the Holy Eucharist transubstantiation   Mystery of Faith Real Presence   tabernacle   sacrilege

Q. 159 *What is the Eucharist?*
The Eucharist is the sacrament that contains the Body, Blood, Soul, and Divinity of our Lord Jesus Christ, under the appearances of bread and wine (CCC 1333).

Q. 160 *When did Jesus Christ institute the Eucharist?*
Jesus Christ instituted the Eucharist at the Last Supper, when he consecrated and changed bread and wine into his Body and Blood and distributed it to the apostles, commanding them to "do this in memory of me" (CCC 1337, 1339).

Q. 161 *Why did Jesus Christ institute the Eucharist?*

Jesus Christ instituted the Eucharist to be a perpetual Sacrifice of the New Covenant, memorial of his Passion, death, and Resurrection, and spiritual food to nourish his Church (CCC 1341, 1365, 1382).

Q. 162 *Is the same Jesus Christ present in the Eucharist who was born on earth of the Virgin Mary?*

Yes, the same Jesus Christ is present in the Eucharist who was born on earth of the Virgin Mary (CCC 1373–75).

Q. 163 *What is the Host before the Consecration?*

Before the Consecration, the Host is bread (CCC 1376).

Q. 164 *What is the Host after the Consecration?*

After the Consecration, the Host is the true Body, Blood, Soul, and Divinity of our Lord Jesus Christ under the appearance of bread (CCC 1376).

Q. 165 *What is contained in the chalice before the Consecration?*

Before the Consecration, wine and a small amount of water are contained in the chalice (CCC 1376).

Q. 166 *What is contained in the chalice after the Consecration?*

After the Consecration, the Body, Blood, Soul, and Divinity of our Lord Jesus Christ is contained in the chalice under the appearance of wine (CCC 1376).

Q. 167 *When do the bread and wine become the Body, Blood, Soul, and Divinity of our Lord Jesus Christ?*

The bread and wine become the Body, Blood, Soul, and Divinity of our Lord Jesus Christ at the moment of the Consecration (CCC 1353, 1376).

Q. 168 *After the Consecration, is there anything left of the bread and the wine?*

After the Consecration, the appearances of bread and wine remain, without their substance, so that what is really present is Jesus Christ, Body, Blood, Soul, and Divinity (CCC 1374–75).

Q. 169 *What effects does the Eucharist produce in him who receives it worthily?*

In him who receives it worthily, the Holy Eucharist preserves, increases, and renews the life of grace; forgives venial sins and strengthens us against future sins; and gives us joy and consolation by increasing charity and hope of eternal life (CCC 1392, 1394, 1402).

Q. 170 *What do we call the change from bread and wine into the Body, Blood, Soul, and Divinity of our Lord Jesus Christ?*

The change from bread and wine into the Body, Blood, Soul, and Divinity of our Lord Jesus Christ is called transubstantiation (CCC 1376).

CHAPTER 22

The Eucharistic Sacrifice

How much more shall the blood of Christ, who through the eternal Spirit offered himself without blemish to God, purify your conscience from dead works to serve the living God. Therefore he is the mediator of a new covenant, so that those who are called may receive the promised eternal inheritance, since a death has occurred which redeems them from the transgressions under the first covenant.

Hebrews 9:14–15

As a sacrament, we think of the Eucharist as a holy meal which Jesus told us to celebrate

in memory of him. The Mass looks like a meal for it has a table (altar) covered with a cloth, bread, wine, water, and people praying, eating, and drinking together as one family in Christ.

But the Mass is also a Sacrifice. It has everything that is required for this act of worship to God: an altar dedicated for sacrifice, a priest who does the offering, and precious gifts to be offered. At the Last Supper, Jesus made the Mass a spiritual reliving of his Sacrifice on the Cross. How? By the words he used. Think about the most important words at Mass, the **words of Consecration** which come to us from Christ himself:

> This is my Body which will be *given up* for you.

> This is the cup of my Blood, the Blood of the new and everlasting covenant. It will be *shed for you and for all* so that sins may be forgiven.

See how they remind us of a sacrifice—a body to be given up and blood to be shed? Of course Jesus was talking about his sacrifice on the Cross; but the Mass he gave us is closely connected with it. The **Sacrifice of the Mass** is not a *new* sacrifice or *another* sacrifice. It is really the same one that Jesus offered once for all upon the Cross. How can this be? In both events there is only one priest doing the offering (Jesus) and there is only one victim or gift being offered (Jesus). So if you have the same priest and the very same offering, it must be the same sacrifice! This is hard to understand, but again we must remind ourselves that it is a mystery that we believe by faith.

The Sacrifice of the Mass

Of course there is some difference in the way the sacrifice of Jesus was offered on the Cross and in the Eucharist.

Upon the Cross, Jesus offered himself in pain and bloody suffering. In the Mass he offers his Body and Blood without pain, under the appearances of the consecrated bread and wine. But it is the same Jesus.

Also, upon the Cross Jesus offered his sacrifice by himself. At Mass he offers it with his Church—through the priest and the congregation.

Saint Paul reminds us that the Eucharist is a reliving of the sacrifice of the Cross. In his first letter to the Corinthians he tells us: "For as often as you eat this bread and drink the cup, you proclaim the Lord's death until he comes" (1 Cor 11:26).

We can also see that the Mass is a sacrifice by looking at the prayers used during its celebration:

Lord God, we ask you to receive us and be pleased with *the sacrifice we offer you* with humble and contrite hearts (Priest's Offertory prayer).

May the Lord accept the *sacrifice at your hands* for the praise and glory of his name, for our good, and the good of all his Church (People's Offertory prayer).

We offer to you, God of glory and majesty, this *holy and perfect sacrifice*: the bread of life and the cup of eternal salvation (Eucharistic Prayer I).

Lord, may this *sacrifice*, which has made our peace with you, advance the peace and salvation of all the world (Eucharistic Prayer III).

Looking forward to his coming in glory, we offer you his body and blood, *the acceptable sacrifice* which brings salvation to the whole world (Eucharistic Prayer IV).

The Mass in Our Lives

The Mass, or celebration of the Eucharist, is the greatest worship we can offer to God. If we remember that being at Mass is very much like standing with Our Lady beneath the Cross of Jesus, we will be sure to pray with love and devotion.

You may hear someone say that he "doesn't get anything out of" the Mass. First of all, we should never look upon the Mass as something we go to in order to "get" something. But we will get more from Mass if we put something of ourselves into it. If you want the Mass to help you grow in your friendship with Christ you must *prepare* yourself for it every week.

Preparing for Mass

1. One good way to prepare for Mass is to go to confession frequently to receive God's help in overcoming your faults.

2. Spend a few minutes reading the Gospel passage that will be used at Mass. This will help you to learn about Jesus and his teachings.

3. Get to church a few minutes *before* Mass begins and ask the Blessed Virgin Mary to help you pray the Mass with faith, hope, and love.

4. Finally, do not rush out of church after Mass but try to spend a few minutes in private prayer with Jesus, whom you have just received. Speak to him in your own words as you would to a best friend, for he wants to be that to you.

Q. 171 *Is the Eucharist only a sacrament?*

No, the Eucharist is not only a sacrament; it is also the permanent Sacrifice of the new covenant (CCC 1367, 1382).

Q. 172 *What is the Holy Mass?*

The Holy Mass is the Sacrifice and sacred Meal of the Body and Blood of Jesus Christ, which is offered on the altar by the priest to God under the appearances of bread and wine, in memory of the sacrifice of the Cross and in renewal of that same sacrifice (CCC 1367, 1382).

Q. 173 *Is the Sacrifice of the Mass the same sacrifice as the sacrifice of the Cross?*

The Sacrifice of the Mass is the same sacrifice as the sacrifice of the Cross; the only difference is in the manner of offering it (CCC 1366–67).

Q. 174 *What is the difference between the sacrifice of the Cross and the Sacrifice of the Mass?*

On the Cross, Jesus Christ offered himself in a bloody manner; on the altar, Jesus Christ offers himself in an unbloody manner, by the ministry of the priest (CCC 1367).

Q. 175 *For what purposes is the Mass offered to God?*

The Mass is offered to God to give him the supreme worship of adoration, to thank him for his blessings to us, to make satisfaction for our sin, and to obtain graces for the welfare of the faithful, living and dead (CCC 1368).

CHAPTER 23

The Eucharist in Our Lives

And by that will we have beèn sanctified through the offering of the body of Jesus Christ once for all.

Hebrews 10:10

The Second Vatican Council called the Holy Eucharist the *source* and *summit* of the Christian life. This means that it is the most important part of our faith. Why? Because the Eucharist is not only a way to receive grace but it

is Jesus himself, the source of all grace! There is not one saint in the Church who did not treasure the Blessed Sacrament as the greatest gift of God to the Church. All of these holy men, women, teenagers, and children knew how necessary Holy Communion is for growing in our relationship with Jesus, so they tried to attend Mass as often as possible.

The Eucharist and the Other Sacraments

Because of the Real Presence of Jesus under the appearances of bread and wine, the Eucharist is called the *greatest of sacraments*. As the famous teacher and saint, Thomas Aquinas, said: "The noblest sacrament is that in which Christ's Body is really present. The Eucharist crowns all the other sacraments."

Baptism makes us members of the Church and gives us the right to receive the Eucharist. The gifts of the Holy Spirit, received at Confirmation, help us to know and love the Blessed Sacrament as mature Catholic Christians. Penance takes our sins away and helps us to go to Holy Communion with pure hearts. Anointing strengthens, cleanses, and prepares in a special

way those who are about to receive Jesus for the last time on earth. Holy Orders gives the priest the power to celebrate Mass and change the gifts of bread and wine into the Body, Blood, Soul, and Divinity of Jesus Christ. In Matrimony a husband and wife show their love by giving themselves to each other. This reminds us of the Eucharist in which Jesus shows his love by giving us his Body and Blood.

Receiving the Eucharist Properly

We will grow in grace only by receiving the Blessed Sacrament properly. Someone can go to Communion a hundred times, but if he does not have faith in Jesus and the desire to love him, these Communions will not do him any good. So a very important question is this: How can I best prepare myself to receive Jesus in the Eucharist? The Church has made some wise rules to help us.

First, we must never receive Jesus if we have a mortal sin on our souls. We must first confess to a priest and be freed from this sin. If we have committed venial sins, we should ask God to forgive them during the Penitential Rite of the Mass.

Second, we must have faith in Jesus' Real Presence and tell him that we believe in it. Saint Paul told the Christians in Corinth: "Whoever, therefore, eats the bread or drinks the cup of the Lord in an unworthy manner will be guilty of profaning the body and blood of the Lord. Let a man examine himself, and so eat of the bread and drink of the cup. For any one who eats and drinks without discerning the body eats and drinks judgment upon himself" (1 Cor 11:27–29).

Last, we must keep the **Eucharistic fast**. This means that we do not eat or drink anything (except water or medicine) for *one hour* before receiving Our Lord. This is a small sacrifice we offer to Jesus, to show him that we honor his Body and Blood as special food and drink. (Those who are advanced in age or who suffer from any infirmity, as well as those who take care of them, can receive the Holy Eucharist even if they have taken something during the previous hour.) When we receive Jesus in Holy Communion, we invite him into our lives and unite ourselves to him as an offering to the Father. We are in union with God and should strive to make the time prayerful and attentive.

Devotion to the Blessed Sacrament

Since the Real Presence of Jesus remains in the Blessed Sacrament after Mass, the Eucharist is placed in the tabernacle for safekeeping, for use at other Masses, and for bringing Communion to the sick.

But Jesus is not kept in our churches for "practical" purposes only. He is there so that we can come to him at any time during the week. Whenever we want to adore or thank God, we can go to the church to worship him in the tabernacle. Person to person, we can tell him our needs and ask him to bless our studies, our friendships, our hopes, and our dreams.

Sometimes the Eucharist is taken out of the tabernacle and put into a special container called a **monstrance**. It has a little glass window that allows us to see our Eucharistic Lord in the **Host**, the consecrated bread. Often, a special prayer-service is held during which the priest holds up the monstrance and blesses the people with Jesus. This is called **Benediction**. These signs of love toward the Eucharist are known as *devotions* to the Blessed Sacrament. They are greatly recommended to us by the Pope and the bishops of the Church.

Words to Know:
Eucharistic fast   monstrance
Host   Benediction

Q. 176 *What things are necessary for the worthy reception of Holy Communion?*

For a worthy reception of Holy Communion, three things are necessary: first, to be in the grace of God; second, to recognize and to consider whom we are about to receive; third, to observe the Eucharistic fast (CCC 1385, 1387).

Q. 177 *What does it mean "to be in the grace of God"?*

"To be in the grace of God" means to have one's soul free from all mortal sin (CCC 1385).

Q. 178 *If a person receives Holy Communion knowing that he is in mortal sin, does he receive Jesus Christ?*

He who receives Holy Communion knowing that he is in mortal sin, does indeed receive Jesus Christ, but not his grace. In fact, he commits a sacrilege, another mortal sin (CCC 1385).

Q. 179 *What does it mean to "recognize and to consider whom one is about to receive"?*

To "recognize and to consider whom one is about to receive" means that we should approach our Lord Jesus Christ in the Eucharist with a living faith, with an ardent desire, and with deep humility and modesty (CCC 1386).

Q. 180 *What does the Eucharistic fast require?*

The Eucharistic fast requires one who is to receive the Holy Eucharist to abstain from any food or drink (except water and medicine) for one hour before Holy Communion (CCC 1387, CIC 919, §1).

Q. 181 *In danger of death, may one receive Holy Communion without fasting?*

Yes, in danger of death, one may receive Holy Communion without fasting (CCC 1387).

Q. 182 *Is there an obligation to receive Holy Communion?*

Yes, there is an obligation to receive Holy Communion at least once a year during the Easter season (CCC 1389).

Q. 183 *Is it beneficial to receive Holy Communion frequently?*

It is beneficial to receive Holy Communion frequently, even every day, provided one has the proper dispositions (CCC 1389).

Q. 184 *Why is the Most Holy Eucharist kept in the churches?*

The Most Holy Eucharist is kept in the churches so that the faithful may adore the Eucharist, and so that it is available for Holy Communion (CCC 1378–79).

CHAPTER 24

Sin and Mankind

And lead us not into temptation, But deliver us from evil.

Matthew 6:13

In Chapter 3 we learned that when God had created the first human beings he gave them sanctifying grace and other special gifts. But Adam and Eve sinned by disobeying God. As a result, they lost the gift of God's life in their souls. They now found it very difficult to obey God's commands because sin made selfishness rule in their hearts. We, the descendants of Adam and Eve, share in this same difficulty. We all experience the frustration of a *fallen* human nature, that is, a body and soul that are weakened because of sin. Saint Paul revealed how much this bothered him:

> I do not understand my own actions. For I do not do what I want, but I do the very thing I hate. Now if I do what I do not want, I agree that the law is good. So then it is no longer I that do it, but sin which dwells within me. For I know that nothing good dwells within me, that is, in my flesh. I can will what is right, but I cannot do it. For I do not do the good I want, but the evil I do not want is what I do (Rom 7:15–19).

Like this great saint and apostle, so often we cannot understand our behavior. Why did I disobey my parents? Why did I lie to my friends? Why does it seem to be so hard to obey the Ten Commandments? The answer to these questions can be summed up in two words: original sin. It has weakened us and inclines us to choose our own desires over those of God. It leads us to think of ourselves as the most important person in existence. In other words, it is nothing but bad news.

But Jesus brought us good news—the news that we can be free of original sin and overcome its bad effects! All we have to do is receive him and share in his life of grace. We do this when we accept Baptism, receive the sacraments, obey his teachings, and grow in prayer. He will do the rest. But there are still a few things that we have to watch out for as we try to live this life in Christ: **temptation** and **sin**.

The False Promises of Temptation

Temptation is the enticement to sin. It always comes before sin and tells us that what is wrong will actually be good for us. There are three things that lead us into temptation: the world, the flesh, and the devil.

The *world* means those persons or created things that lure us away from Jesus' teachings. Perhaps you have a friend who leads you to sin. Whenever you are with him you seem to do more wrong than usual. In your heart you know he is a bad influence on you. This person would be one example of how we are tempted by "the world."

The *flesh* means our own inner urges. There are seven basic disordered inclinations that lead us to sin. These are called the *capital* sins because they stand at the head of other sins.

PRIDE: An exaggerated opinion of oneself.

AVARICE: An uncontrolled desire for earthly goods, such as money, clothes, etc.

ENVY: Unhappiness or discontent over the good fortune or success of others.

WRATH: An uncontrolled feeling of displeasure and antagonism.

LUST: An uncontrolled desire for sexual pleasure.

GLUTTONY: An uncontrolled use of food and drink.

SLOTH: Laziness or carelessness in doing right and practicing virtue because of the work and effort needed to do so.

The *devil* means satan and the other bad angels who try to make us disobey God and who hate the Christian life. Saint Peter warned all believers to be on guard against satan and his spiritual attacks: "Be sober, be watchful. Your adversary the devil prowls around like a roaring lion, seeking some one to devour. Resist him, firm in your faith, knowing that the same experience of suffering is required of your brotherhood throughout the world" (1 Pet 5:8–9).

Temptations often come to us through **occasions of sin**. These are persons, places, or things that may easily cause us to sin. Some examples are: friends who do not respect religion; movies or magazines that promote sexual excess and the wrong use of our sexual powers; parties at which drugs and alcohol are abused. The first step in overcoming sin is to know what leads you into it. Then you will know what or whom to avoid if you really want to reach heaven.

Sin and Its Evil Effects

Sin is an offense against God in thought, word, action, or neglect of action (omission). For example, a real hatred for someone in your mind is a sin of thought. Using God's name disrespectfully is a sin by word. Getting drunk or stealing something would be a sin by action. Not going to Sunday Mass without a good reason (such as illness) would be a sin by omission or neglect of action.

There are two kinds of sin, original and actual. Original sin, as we have seen, means the first offense committed by Adam. We all share in it because we are all his physical descendants. *Actual sins* are those which we personally commit. Actual sins can be either *mortal* or *venial*.

Mortal sin is the worst evil there is in the world because it kills God's life within us. Think about the most terrible evils there are on earth: wars, floods, earthquakes, disease, etc. None of these are as bad as a mortal sin. Why? Because they can only kill the body, as horrible as that can be. Mortal sin, however, kills the supernatural life of the soul and takes away the possibility of entering heaven. The person who dies in mortal sin sends himself to hell. This is because even one mortal sin tells God that we want nothing to do with him or his holy law. And God respects our free will. He will allow us to suffer forever in hell if that is what we choose.

Since this is such a terrible evil, it is very important that we know what makes something a mortal sin. There are three things that make a sin mortal:

1. The offense must be *seriously wrong*, or at least we think it is seriously wrong. Seriously to disobey the Ten Commandments or the teachings and laws of the Church is a mortal sin. For example, missing Mass on Sunday is a mortal sin unless we have a good reason such as illness or no church in the area. It is seriously wrong because God commands us to worship him and the Church says that we do this by assisting at Mass on Sunday.

2. We must *know clearly* that what we chose to think, do, say, or not do is seriously wrong. For example, if you did not know that Sunday Mass was a serious duty, then you did not commit a mortal sin by not attending.

3. We must *freely choose* to commit the sin. Continuing with the example of Sunday Mass, if we do not go to Mass because the car breaks down on the way to church, we do not choose not to go. In this case we do not commit a sin. However, if we decide not to get out of bed in time for Mass, we freely choose not to go. In this case, we commit mortal sin.

Venial sins are offenses that are not serious violations of God's holy law. They weaken our relationship with God, but they do not destroy it as mortal sins do. We should try to do away with these smaller sins, however, because they can form a bad attitude in us and even lead us to commit worse sins. "Venial" means "forgivable." These lesser sins do not take grace away. Venial sins may be forgiven by repentance and good works, even without sacramental confession. It is still very good to confess all sins, even the smallest. This helps us to eliminate sinful habits and desires. We should strive to love God so perfectly that we will not offend him even in small ways.

The Role of Conscience

The Catholic Church has always said that men must follow their consciences in order to do good and avoid sin. By **conscience** we mean the ability everyone has to judge right from wrong in human actions.

Since we are to act in accord with our consciences it is very important for us to form a *good* conscience. We do this by learning what the Church teaches and by listening to those whom God has placed over us to guide us, such as our parents, our priests, and our teachers. If you are confused about what is right or wrong, you should ask your parents or a priest about it. Growth in knowing what is good from what is evil is an important part of the Sacrament of Penance.

Words to Know:

sin   temptation   occasion of sin
mortal sin   venial sin   conscience

Q. 185   *What is sin?*
Sin is an offense done to God by disobeying his law (CCC 1849–50).

Q. 186   *What is mortal sin?*
Mortal sin is an act of disobedience to the law of God in a serious matter, done with full knowledge and deliberate consent (CCC 1857).

Q. 187   *What are the effects of mortal sin?*
Mortal sin destroys grace and charity in the soul and turns us away from God and heaven (CCC 1855–56).

Q. 188   *What is venial sin?*
Venial sin is an act of disobedience to the law of God in a lesser matter, or in a matter in itself serious, but done without full knowledge or consent (CCC 1862).

Q. 189   *Why is a sin that is less serious called "venial?"*
A less serious sin is called "venial" that is, forgivable, because it does not take grace away and because it can be forgiven by repentance and good works, even without sacramental confession (CCC 1855).

Q. 190   *What is an occasion of sin?*
An occasion of sin is any person, circumstance, or thing that puts us in danger of sinning.

Q. 191   *Are we obliged to avoid the occasions of sin?*
Yes, we are obliged to avoid the occasions of sin because we are obliged to avoid sin itself.

CHAPTER 25

God's Mercy and Forgiveness

I confess my iniquity, I am sorry for my sin.

Psalm 38:18

In Jesus' time some of the religious leaders of the Jews seemed to forget the loving forgiveness that God had shown their ancestors. Instead, they kept reminding the people only about God's *justice*, especially that he punishes every sin that we commit. They spoke of God as if he were a merciless judge who found joy in condemning everyone—except the most learned and religious of people!

But when Jesus preached to these people he told them that God is full of *mercy* and *forgiveness*. **Mercy** means that God has love and tenderness toward weak mankind. Our Lord, God-become-man, showed this mercy in his dealings with sinners.

When sinners came to Jesus he never ignored them or treated them as outcasts. He made them feel wanted and loved, and he made friends with them. He even called one of them, Matthew, to be an apostle; and another, Mary Magdalene, to be one of his closest disciples! Jesus' kind attitude toward sinners made the leaders of the Jews very upset. One day they complained to his disciples: "Why does your teacher eat with tax collectors and sinners?" (Mt 9:11).

Jesus overheard this remark and said to them: "Those who are well have no need of a physician, but those who are sick. Go and learn what this means, 'I desire mercy, and not sacrifice.' For I came not to call the righteous, but sinners" (Mt 9:12–13).

What Jesus meant was that he was like a doctor who is concerned with the health of people. He is the Divine Physician who has come to heal the sickness of sin in our souls. He has come to offer forgiveness and freedom from sin to each one of us.

God Loves the Sinner but Hates the Sin

Some people think that the friendships which Jesus made with sinners mean that he approved of their sinful desires and actions. This is far from the truth! He loved each person because he was created by God, who commands us to love all men. But he hated each sin and never told anyone that he approved of his sinfulness. Do you remember the story in the Gospel about the woman caught in the act of adultery? Some of the scribes and pharisees were about to kill this woman. But Jesus reminded them that they, too, were guilty of sins. Then he said to her, "Go, and do not sin again" (Jn 8:11).

We All Need a Change of Heart

Like the woman mentioned above, all of us stand before Jesus as sinners who come to him for forgiveness. We go to him in confession and leave the sacrament freed from sin. How can we "go and sin no more?" By having a **change of heart**. This means that we honestly try to do good and avoid committing sin, even when it is difficult. It means that we try to see things as Jesus would: giving first place in life to God, second to our neighbor, and last to ourselves.

One of the ways to have a change of heart is to spend a few minutes at night thinking about the way we spent our day. We briefly review the Ten Commandments to see if we have been faithful in obeying them. This time of reflection helps us to know which sins we commit and how often we commit them. This also helps us to avoid sins in the future. There is a very good Christian practice called the **examination of conscience** that helps us to discover our sins and work on a change of heart. You can find an examination of conscience at the end of this book.

When you examine your conscience, you should consider the price Jesus paid for your sins, how they offend God, and how they hurt your neighbors. You should be sorry for your sins. This is called contrition. There are two kinds of sorrow for sin: perfect contrition, which means that we are sorry for our sins because they offend God, whom we should love above all things, and imperfect contrition, also called "attrition," which means that we are sorry for our sins because we fear punishment for them. Both kinds of sorrow for sin

are acceptable for confession, but perfect contrition is the better form of sorrow for sin.

Another way of growing in this change of heart is to remember that at death we will have to stand before God and be judged. Then there will be no more time for us to change our way of life. When we die, we will be sent to one of three spiritual places: heaven, purgatory, or hell. Heaven is rewarded to those who have died in God's grace and tried to know, love, and serve God with all their heart and with all their strength. It is eternal happiness in God's presence. Purgatory is for those who wanted to love God and serve him on earth, but who nevertheless did not really try as hard as they could have. They died with venial sins or temporal punishment due to sin. In this state, they are purified of their venial sins or punishment for sin and prepared for heaven. Hell is for those who rejected God and died in a state of mortal sin. In life they tried to satisfy their selfish desires, did not repent of their sins, and refused to accept God's mercy. Hell is the absence of God and a place of eternal punishment for those who choose by their actions to reject God. The souls in hell are separated from God forever.

Once we have considered our sins by an examination of conscience and have sorrow for our sins, we must have a purpose of amendment. To have a firm purpose of amendment is not to sin again and to avoid that which may lead us to sin.

The best way to change our hearts is to receive the Sacrament of Penance often, at least once a month. In this way we will have our sins forgiven, and we will receive the strength we need to avoid them in the future. Although confession is *necessary* only when we have committed a mortal sin, confessing our venial sins gives us grace, which helps us to avoid the sins we have confessed, even those that are venial. The priest will also give us good advice on how to become a better Christian.

Take up Your Cross and Follow Me

One day, Jesus said to his disciples: "If any man would come after me, let him deny himself and take up his cross and follow me" (Mt 16:24).

He calls us to do the same thing. This means that we must learn to deny our selfish desires by doing little acts of **penance**. Some examples of penance are not eating between meals or volunteering to do the dishes after dinner even if it is not your turn to wash them. By doing little things that are not appealing to us for the love of God, we strengthen our wills. Then, when temptations to sin come along, we will be better prepared to say "no" to them.

Saint Dominic Savio, the popular teenager we read about in Chapter 15, was able to accomplish a change of heart in this way. He learned to hate sin and love God by examining his conscience nightly, by going to confession weekly, by receiving the Eucharist often, and by denying his selfish desires through acts of penance. You can have a change of heart too!

Words to Know:
mercy   change of heart
examination of conscience   penance

Q. 192 *How is the examination of conscience made?*

The examination of conscience is made by calling to mind the sins we have committed (in thought, word, act, or omission) against the Commandments of God, against the Precepts of the Church, and against the obligations to our state in life (CCC 1454).

Q. 193 *What is contrition?*

Contrition is sorrow and hatred for our sins and the resolution not to sin again (CCC 1451–53).

Q. 194 *How many kinds of contrition are there?*

There are two kinds of contrition: perfect and imperfect (CCC 1452–53).

Q. 195 *What is perfect contrition?*

Perfect contrition is sorrow for sin that results from love of God above all things and includes a hatred of the sins we have committed because they offend God (CCC 1452).

Q. 196 *What is imperfect contrition?*

Imperfect contrition is sorrow for sin that results from the fear of punishments for sin, or from the ugliness of sin (CCC 1453).

Q. 197 *Should we have contrition for all the sins we have committed?*

Yes, we should have contrition for all the sins we have committed (CCC 1453).

Q. 198 *What is the purpose of amendment?*

The purpose of amendment is the steadfast will not to sin again and to avoid the occasions of sin (CCC 1451).

CHAPTER 26

The Sacrament of Penance

If we confess our sins, he is faithful and just, and will forgive our sins and cleanse us from all unrighteousness.

1 John 1:9

God calls each one of us to receive new life in him, the life of sanctifying grace. We first received this life in the holy waters of Baptism, which takes away sin and makes us temples of the Holy Spirit. But what about the sins we commit *after* Baptism? How can we be washed clean again? By the wonderful Sacrament of Penance (also called confession and reconciliation)—the gift of God's love and mercy to his people.

On the night he rose from the dead, Jesus appeared to his apostles and gave them the priestly power to celebrate this sacrament. Saint John, who was an eyewitness at this event, describes it for us:

> On the evening of that day, the first day of the week, the doors being shut where the disciples were, for fear of the Jews, Jesus came and stood among them and said to them, "Peace be with you." When he had said this, he showed them his hands and his side. Then the disciples were glad when they saw the Lord. Jesus said to them again, "Peace be with you. As the Father has sent me, even so I send you." And when he had said this, he breathed on them, and said to them, "Receive the Holy Spirit. If you forgive the sins of any, they are forgiven; if you re-tain the sins of any, they are retained" (Jn 20:19–23).

By these words Jesus gave the apostles the power to forgive sins, something only God can do! How can this be? Because Our Lord shared with them his mission as Savior. They were to go throughout the world forgiving sins just as he had done. Christ had shared his teaching authority with them and also gave them the power (at the Last Supper) to change bread and wine into his Body and Blood, so now he gives them the power to forgive sins. Saint Paul reminded the early Christians about this power of the priesthood: "All this is from God, who through Christ reconciled us to himself and gave us the ministry of reconciliation; that is, God was in Christ reconciling the world to himself, not counting their trespasses against them, and entrusting to us the message of reconciliation. So we are ambassadors for Christ, God making his appeal through us" (2 Cor 5:18–20).

Understanding the Sacrament of Penance

We can better understand this sacrament by looking more closely at the words Jesus used when he gave it to the Church.

"Peace be with you": This tells us that Jesus was giving the sacrament as a way to have true peace in our lives. Through it he takes away our sins. This helps us to free our guilty conscience which robs the soul of inner peace.

"As the Father has sent me": This reminds us that Jesus was the ambassador of God the Father. An ambassador is someone who is sent by someone else with an important message to deliver. The message Jesus brought to us was the good news of salvation—the truth that we can be saved from our sins and from hell if we follow him.

"So I send you": This reminds us of the passage we just read from Saint Paul, where he calls himself and other priests "Ambassadors of Christ." As the Father had sent Jesus to take away sins, so now Jesus sends his priests to do the same thing.

"Receive the Holy Spirit": You will remember from the chapter on Confirmation that the Spirit is full of *power*. This is the power of God which alone can take away sins. When we go to confession, the priest forgives our sins by the power of the Holy Spirit. He cannot do this on his own because he is a sinful man just as we are, but as a priest he has this power.

"If you forgive men's sins, they are forgiven them": This tells us that Jesus *did* give the ministry of forgiveness and reconciliation to the apostles. They, in turn, passed this work on to other priests down to our own day. We do not have to wonder whether God forgives us when we go to confession, for we have Jesus' word that he does!

"If you hold them bound, they are held bound": This reminds us that the priest can also *refuse* to forgive us our sins. If he asks us to give up a sinful action and we say "no," then he will not give us absolution. Why? Because this shows that we are not really sorry for the sin, and we still want to commit it. Our sins can be forgiven only if we are truly sorry and promise to avoid them in the future.

The Sign and Effects of Penance

As with all the sacraments, Penance has its own sign. The **sign of Penance** is, first, the **confession of sins**, or telling of sins to the priest, and, second, the words of **absolution**, or forgiveness, which the priest says while making the Sign of the Cross over us.

The sign tells us what effects this sacrament has on our souls. The sign of our private confession shows that the sins we are revealing will be taken away. The sign of absolution tells us that they *are* taken away. The cross which the priest makes over us with his hands reminds us that sins can be forgiven only because Jesus died on the Cross for them.

If we have properly prepared ourselves for this sacrament, God does wonderful things for us.

First, he takes away the sins we have confessed and restores the life of grace to our souls if we had lost it by mortal sin. If we had only venial sins to confess, God increases his grace within us and strengthens our friendship with him. So you can see that it is good to receive this sacrament even when we have not broken off our life with God by mortal sin.

Second, he even takes away the punishment our sins deserve. Of course, this punishment is taken away according to how great our sorrow is and how determined we are to avoid sin in the future. It is similar to the punishment we receive from our parents when we disobey them. If they see that we are really sorry for having gone against their wishes and that we are trying to make up for our disobedience, they may shorten our punishment or even cancel it altogether. With sin, we can either make up for it in this life by prayer and acts of penance or in the next life by being purified in purgatory.

Last, in the Sacrament of Penance God gives us all the actual graces we need in order to do good and avoid sin in the future. He rewards our honesty in going to confession by giving us the help we need to overcome the sinful desires and actions we have confessed. For example, if you confess to lying and committing impure actions, God will give you even more strength to be truthful and pure in the days ahead.

How to Make a Good Confession

You need to do five things in order to make a good confession:

1. *Examine your conscience* before receiving the sacrament. This helps you to recognize all of your sins clearly.

2. *Have sorrow for having sinned.* We should pray that God will help us to have perfect contrition for our sins. We must have at least imperfect contrition (attrition) for our sins to make a good confession.

3. *Make a firm resolution to do all you can to avoid sin and occasions of sin in the future.* If you are truly sorry for your sins, you will strive not to sin again.

4. *Confess your sins (accuse yourself of your sins) to the priest honestly, not trying to hide anything out of shame or embarrassment.* Remember that the priest will not yell at you or think you are a terrible person. He is there to give you God's forgiveness, and he is glad that you have had the honesty and courage to come to the sacrament. The priest may never reveal what you confess to anyone. What you make known to the priest in Confession remains "sealed" by the Sacrament of Penance. This absolute and unbreakable secrecy is called the "seal of confession."

5. *Receive absolution and do the penance which the priest gives you.* This is usually a few prayers or a good deed to help to make up for the selfishness of your sins. You should do your penance as soon as possible.

The Rite of Penance

Like the other sacraments, there is a special rite, or ceremony, involved in the celebration of Penance. Whether you go to confession "face to face" or privately, it always follows this general plan.

First, upon entering the **confessional**, the priest will greet you. You make the Sign of the Cross while saying the words that go with it: "In the Name of the Father, and of the Son, and of the Holy Spirit. *Amen.*"

Then the priest may read a short passage

from the Bible, or he may simply tell you to begin confessing your sins. You start by saying how long it has been since your last confession. Then you reveal your sins, the mortal ones first, if you have committed any. You must tell the priest how many times you committed a sin and any information that is relevant. If you cannot remember the number of your mortal sins you must indicate to the confessor the number that is closest to the truth.

After you have finished confessing, the priest will give you some advice on living a better Christian life. At this time he will also give you your penance. If it is prayer, you should say it before you leave the church. If it is a good deed, try to do it as soon as possible.

Before giving you absolution, he will ask you to show your sorrow by reciting an **Act of Contrition**. He will then say the words of forgiveness:

God, the Father of mercies, through the death and Resurrection of his Son has reconciled the world to himself and sent the Holy Spirit among us for the forgiveness of sins; through the ministry of the Church may God give you pardon and peace, and I absolve you from your sins, in the Name of the Father, and of the Son, and of the Holy Spirit. *Amen.*

He will say goodbye to you with a short prayer that says: "Give thanks to the Lord, for he is good." And you reply: "His mercy endures for ever."

Words to Know:

sign of Penance
confession of sins   absolution
confessional   Act of Contrition

Q. 199 *What is the Sacrament of Penance?*
The Sacrament of Penance (also called confession and reconciliation) is the sacrament instituted by Jesus Christ to forgive the sins committed after Baptism (CCC 1422, 1425).

Q. 200 *When was the Sacrament of Penance instituted by Jesus Christ?*
The Sacrament of Penance was instituted by Jesus Christ when he said to the apostles, and through them to their successors: "Receive the Holy Spirit. If you forgive the sins of any, they are forgiven; if you retain the sins of any, they are retained" (CCC 1442–44, Jn 20:22–23).

Q. 201 *Who is the minister of the Sacrament of Penance?*
The minister of the Sacrament of Penance is a priest approved by the bishop (CCC 1444).

Q. 202 *What is required to make a good confession?*

Five things are required to make a good confession: 1) examination of conscience, 2) sorrow for sin, 3) intention not to sin again, 4) accusation of sins to a priest, and 5) reception of absolution and penance (CCC 1451, 1454-55, 1459).

Q. 203 *What is the accusation of sins?*

The accusation of sins is the declaration of our sins made to the priest (CCC 1456).

Q. 204 *Which sins are we obliged to confess?*

We are obliged to confess all mortal sins that have not been confessed yet, or which were not confessed the right way (CCC 1456).

Q. 205 *How should we accuse ourselves of our mortal sins?*

We should accuse ourselves of every remembered mortal sin according to kind and number, and any important circumstances that may have affected to our guilt (CCC 1455–56).

Q. 206 *What should a person do if he does not remember the precise number of his mortal sins?*

He who does not remember the precise number of his mortal sins should indicate to the confessor the number that seems closest to the truth (CCC 1456).

Q. 207 *Why must we not allow ourselves to hide a mortal sin through shame?*

We must not allow ourselves to hide a mortal sin through shame because we are confessing to Jesus Christ in the person of the priest-confessor (CCC 1455–56).

Q. 208 *Does he make a good confession who unwittingly omits or forgets a mortal sin?*

Yes, he who unwittingly omits or forgets a mortal sin makes a good confession. When the sin is remembered, the obligation remains to confess it at his next opportunity (CCC 1456).

Q. 209 *What must one do if he has made a bad confession?*

He who knows that he did not make a good confession must confess again and accuse himself of his bad confession (CCC 1456).

Q. 210 *Can a priest ever tell anyone your sins?*

No, a priest may not reveal any sin confessed in the Sacrament of Penance even at the cost of his own life (CCC 1467, 2490).

Q. 211 *What is absolution?*

Absolution is the pardoning of the penitent's sins by Jesus Christ, through the priest who says: "I absolve you from your sins in the name of the Father, and of the Son, and of the Holy Spirit." (CCC 1449).

Q. 212 *When sins have been forgiven by absolution, is all punishment for sin also taken away?*

When sins have been taken away by absolution, there remains a debt of temporal punishment to be undergone either in this life or in purgatory (CCC 1472–73).

Q. 213 *What is the "satisfaction," or the penance given in the Sacrament of Penance?*

The satisfaction or penance given is an action, usually a good work or prayers, imposed by the confessor on the penitent in order, by the grace of Christ, to make up for sin (CCC 1459–60).

Q. 214 *When is it proper to do the penance given in the Sacrament of Penance?*

It is fitting to do the penance as soon as possible, unless the confessor has assigned a particular time for it (CCC 1460).

CHAPTER 27

The Sacrament of the Anointing of the Sick

The LORD sustains him on his sickbed; in his illness thou healest all his infirmities.

Psalm 41:3

The very first book of the Bible teaches us that suffering and sickness are the result of original sin. Before this sin, Adam and Eve were kept free from pain, illness, and death.

When Jesus came to earth he showed special love and kindness for the sick and dying. Many of his miracles were performed for these suffering people. He gave sight to the blind, speech to the mute, strong muscles to the paralyzed, and he even raised the dead to life. Can you imagine the joy that leapt up in the people's hearts as they saw their sick friends cured or their paralyzed relatives walking? Truly good news *has* come to us, they must have exclaimed!

But more important to Jesus was the curing of souls. For reasons known to himself he did not cure everyone. To show that he did not abandon the sick and suffering Jesus gave us the Sacrament of the Anointing of the Sick, also called the Sacrament of the Sick. Through this sacrament Jesus gives to the Church's suffering members the spiritual aid to enable them to use their pain for their spiritual perfection, to heal them if it is God's will, and to prepare them for a holy death when the time comes.

Jesus Shares His Healing Power

During his ministry on earth Jesus shared his healing power with his disciples. Saint Mark, who was a close friend of the Apostle Peter, tells us about this:

And he called to him the twelve, and began to send them out two by two, and gave them authority over the unclean spirits. . . . So they went out and preached that men should repent. And they cast out many demons, and anointed with oil many that were sick and healed them (Mk 6:7, 12–13).

After his Resurrection, Jesus' disciples continued to use this healing power in the Sacrament of the Anointing of the Sick. The letter of Saint James tells us that the priests would use holy oil and special prayers to forgive the sins of the sick and even to restore them to health:

Is any among you sick? Let him call for the elders of the church, and let them pray over him, anointing him with oil in the name of the Lord; and the prayer of faith will save the sick man, and the Lord

will raise him up; and if he has committed sins, he will be forgiven (Jas 5:14–15).

Many Catholics do not realize that this sacrament has the power to cure them in body as well as soul. Of course, this would depend upon the plan that God has for the sick person's life. Perhaps the suffering a person experiences helps him to do penance for his sins so that he can go straight to heaven when he dies. Or maybe it is simply his time to leave this earth and go to his true home with God. But the fact remains that many priests have witnessed actual bodily cures as a result of the Sacrament of the Anointing of the Sick.

The Purpose of This Sacrament

For the first twelve hundred years of Christianity, this sacrament was seen as one of healing for both body and soul. Catholics received it whenever they were seriously ill or in danger of death.

But then some people began to develop a strange attitude toward Anointing. They saw it as a sure sign of death, and so they would not call a priest to anoint their sick relatives! They would put the sacrament off until the last moment of life, and it began to be called the "Last Rites."

In our day the Church wants us to understand that Anointing is not to be feared or put off until death is certain. It is meant to help a person prepare for *possible* death by taking away sins and giving peace to the soul. It helps the person who receives it to accept God's plan for his life and to die a holy death if this is God's will. Through this sacrament, the sick and the elderly encounter Jesus, who comes to give them his peace and comfort. The Second Vatican Council told us:

The Sacrament of the Sick should be given, not at the point of death, but as soon as a Christian begins to be in danger of death from sickness or old age (*Sacrosanctum concilium*, III, 73).

The Sign and Effects of Anointing

The special **sign of Annointing** consists of (1) **anointing** with blessed **oil of the sick**, and (2) the following prayer which the priest says while touching the sick person's forehead and hands with the oil:

Through this holy anointing may the Lord in his love and mercy help you with the grace of the Holy Spirit. *Amen.* May the Lord, who frees you from sin, save you and raise you up. *Amen* (Rite of Anointing).

We can tell from this sign what is happening to the person who receives it properly. First, he is strengthened spiritually to accept God's plan for his life. In the early days of the Church, oil was seen as something that gave strength. The Greek athletes would rub it on their muscles before a race or other sports event. Blessed oil is a sign of God's strength and the power of the Holy Spirit. Second, the person's venial sins are forgiven—and his mortal sins if he is unable to confess—which prepares him to go to heaven when he dies. When the priest anoints the forehead, he reminds us to be sorry for sins of thought; the touching of the hands reminds us of those sins committed by deeds.

The Rite of Anointing

The Sacrament of the Anointing of the Sick can be given anywhere: in the hospital, in a church, at the scene of an accident, or in one's home. Let us see how it is celebrated in the house of the sick person.

After the family has called the priest, they should cover a small table or nightstand with a white cloth. On this is put a crucifix, two candles, and a small bowl of water. The priest will bring everything else.

Upon entering the home, the priest calls down God's blessing and sprinkles the sick person's room with holy water. Then he explains the purpose and meaning of the sacrament to the family.

Then, either the sick person receives the Sacrament of Penance or else everyone joins in a penitential rite. After all recite the prayer "I Confess . . ." there is a reading from the Bible that deals with healing and forgiveness. Then it is time for the actual administration of the sacrament. The priest anoints the person with the oil of the sick and says the prayer we have already read. After the anointing he gives Holy Communion to the person and to those present who also wish to receive. The home ceremony closes with a blessing from the priest.

Indulgences

While this sacrament is usually received in old age, we should not wait until then to prepare ourselves for a good and holy death. We can begin now by praying daily, receiving the sacraments often, and storing up for ourselves "treasures in heaven" (Mt 6:20), as Jesus called all of our prayers and good works.

One way we can do this is by gaining **indulgences**.

Indulgences are spiritual riches which shorten or even take away the time we must spend in purgatory making up for our sins. All of our prayers and good works make us more pleasing to God. By saying these prayers or performing these actions devoutly, we show our love for God, and he lessens the punishment we will receive for our past sins. Indulgences can be plenary (which take all our punishment away) or partial (which take some of it away). To obtain an indulgence, we must be in a state of grace and do what is asked, for example, pray the prescribed prayers and do the prescribed good works. To obtain a plenary indulgence, one must also pray for the Holy Father, receive the Sacraments of Penance and Holy Eucharist within eight days, and be detached from all sin, even venial sin.

Words to Know:
> anointing   oil of the sick
> sign of Anointing   indulgence

Q. 215 *What is the Sacrament of the Anointing of the Sick?*
The Anointing of the Sick is the sacrament given to Christians who are gravely ill for their spiritual and bodily strengthening (CCC 1499, 1532).

Q. 216 *Who is the minister of the Sacrament of the Anointing of the Sick?*
The minister of the Sacrament of the Anointing of the Sick is a priest: the pastor of the parish or another priest who has his permission (CCC 1516).

Q. 217 *How does the priest administer the Sacrament of the Anointing of the Sick?*

The priest administers the Anointing of the Sick by anointing the forehead and the hands of the sick person with the oil blessed by the bishop or priest and by saying: "Through this holy anointing may the Lord in his love and mercy help you with the grace of the Holy Spirit. *Amen.* May the Lord, who frees you from sin, save you and raise you up. *Amen*" (CCC 1517–19).

Q. 218 *What effects does the Sacrament of the Anointing of the Sick produce?*

The Sacrament of the Anointing of the Sick increases sanctifying grace. It takes away venial sins and also mortal sins if the sick person is unable to confess them, provided he has sorrow for sin. It gives strength to bear patiently the evil he suffers, to resist temptations, to die a holy death, or, if it is God's will, to regain bodily health (CCC 1520–23).

Q. 219 *When can the Sacrament of the Anointing of the Sick be given?*

The Sacrament of the Anointing of the Sick can be given whenever a person begins to be in danger of death, either on account of a serious illness, a serious injury, or old age (CCC 1514).

Q. 220 *What is an indulgence?*

An indulgence is the remission of the temporal punishment due to sin, which the Church grants under certain conditions to persons in the state of grace (CCC 1471).

Q. 221 *How many kinds of indulgences are there?*

There are two kinds of indulgences: plenary and partial (CCC 1471).

Q. 222 *What is a plenary indulgence?*

A plenary indulgence remits all the temporal punishment due to us for our sins (CCC 1471).

Q. 223 *What is a partial indulgence?*

A partial indulgence remits only a part of the temporal punishment which is due to us for our sins (CCC 1471).

Q. 224 *What is required to obtain indulgences?*

To obtain indulgences, it is necessary that we be in the state of grace and that we carry out the good works prescribed for the indulgence. In order to obtain a plenary indulgence, it is also necessary to: 1) pray for the intentions of the Holy Father, 2) make a sacramental confession and receive the Eucharist within eight days, and 3) have no attachment to venial sin (CCC 1471, 1478).

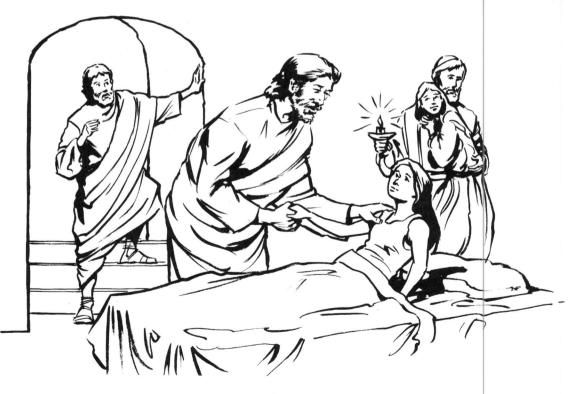

CHAPTER 28

The Sacrament of Holy Orders

I became a minister according to the divine office which was given to me for you, to make the word of God fully known, the mystery hidden for ages and generations but now made manifest to his saints.

Colossians 1:25–26

Up to this point we have studied five sacraments: Baptism, Confirmation, Holy Eucharist, Penance, and Anointing of the Sick. The first three are called *sacraments of initiation*, for they bring us into the Church and give us full participation in it. The other two are known as *sacraments of healing*, because Anointing strengthens in a special way for those who are ill their friendship with God and Penance restores God's life to our souls if we have destroyed it by mortal sin.

In the next two chapters, we shall look at the *sacraments of service*: Holy Orders and Matrimony. They are called sacraments of service because they directly serve or help the salvation of others, rather than those who receive them. Those who receive them are also helped by these sacraments, but this is because the sacraments enable them to help others in important ways. The Sacrament of Holy Orders makes men ordained ministers (bishops, priests, and deacons), who serve others by proclaiming the Word of God, administering the sacraments, and guiding their fellow believers. The sacrament of Holy Matrimony makes a man and a woman husband and wife, who serve others by having children and raising families who will witness to Jesus and the Christian life in the world. In this way, we can see that the sacraments of service give those who receive them a particular mission in the Church. They enable those who receive them to build up the Church as the Body of Christ in particular ways.

Our present chapter is on the Sacrament of Holy Orders. In it we will see how very important Holy Orders are to the Church as those ordained bring salvation to all men.

and the duty of ordaining other worthy men to the priestly ministry. Saint Clement of Rome, who was a friend of the apostles and the fourth Pope, wrote about this passing on of the priesthood:

> The apostles knew, through Our Lord Jesus Christ, that they were to appoint other men to take their place as bishops in the Church. They told these men to choose successors as well.

This passing on of Holy Orders is called **apostolic succession**. It assures us that our Catholic bishops today have received their ministry directly from Jesus through the Twelve. This is why we are able to say that our bishops are the successors of the apostles.

A Royal Nation of Priests

We learn from Saint Peter that all Christians share in the priesthood of Christ. In his first letter to all believers he says: "But you are a chosen race, a royal priesthood, a holy nation, God's own people, that you may declare the wonderful deeds of him who called you out of darkness into his marvelous light" (1 Pet 2:9).

This reminds us that we are all made priests in Baptism, but we must remember that there are different ways of carrying out this common priesthood. Lay people, including Sisters and Brothers in religious communities, carry out their priesthood by attending Mass and by worshipping God through private prayer. This is known as the **priesthood of the faithful**, or the common priesthood. This is different from the **ordained priesthood**, or the ministerial priesthood, which men receive through Holy Orders.

To receive this sacrament, a man must be called by God. This special calling is necessary because a priest's life is very demanding. It can only be lived faithfully by those who are chosen by God to serve him in this way of life.

Jesus Gives Us the Sacrament of Holy Orders

At the Last Supper Jesus made the Twelve Apostles the first priests of his Church. While instituting the Holy Eucharist he said to them: "Do this in remembrance of me" (Lk 22:19).

The command to "do this" meant that Christ had given them a share in his own priestly power so that they could offer the Holy Sacrifice of the Mass. Along with being priests, the Twelve were also made *bishops*. Bishops receive from Jesus the fullness of the priesthood

The Levels in Holy Orders

Most Catholics do not realize that Holy Orders has three different levels. These levels make up the hierarchy of the Church. The word **hierarchy** means "sacred order" and refers to the levels of authority within the Church.

The highest degree of Holy Orders is that of the episcopate, the **bishops**. (Episcopate comes from a Greek word meaning "overseer.") Bishops receive the full power of the priesthood. They are successors to the apostles. This is why only they can ordain men to the priesthood. They are the official teachers of the faith in their *diocese*. Every Catholic owes respect and obedience to the bishop of his diocese.

The next level is the presbyterate, the priesthood. (Presbyterate comes from a Greek word meaning "elder.") Your pastor and his associate **priests** belong to this degree. They are the bishop's helpers in preaching the word of God, teaching the faith, and administering the sacraments. Priests baptize, offer the Eucharistic sacrifice, absolve penitents of their sins, anoint the sick, and witness marriages. With special permission, they sometimes administer the Sacrament of Confirmation in the bishop's place. Every priest makes a promise of obedience to his bishop. The priest is called to become holy because this is the best way of leading others to heaven.

The lowest level in Holy Orders is the deaconate, the **deacons**. (Deaconate comes from a Greek word meaning "minister" or "servant.") Deacons were first ordained in the Church by the apostles, as Saint Luke tells us:

Now in these days when the disciples were increasing in number, the Hellenists murmured against the Hebrews because their widows were neglected in the daily distribution. And the twelve summoned the body of the disciples and said, "It is not right that we should give up preaching the word of God to serve tables. Therefore, brethren, pick out from among you seven men of good repute, full of the Spirit and of wisdom, whom we may appoint to this duty. But we will devote ourselves to prayer and to the ministry of the word." . . . These they set before the apostles, and they prayed and laid their hands upon them (Acts 6:1–6).

This shows us that the deacons are called to serve the Church by carrying out works of mercy. They also help out in parishes by assisting the bishop or priest at Mass, administering Baptism, distributing the Eucharist, assisting at or blessing marriages, officiating at funerals and burial services, and instructing people in the faith. There are two kinds of deacons: those who are studying for the priesthood and those who are called to this way of life as *permanent deacons*. These may be married men who are ordained for service in their own dioceses.

The Sign and Effects of Holy Orders

As we saw in the passage from Saint Luke, the apostles ordained men by praying over them and laying hands upon them. This is how men are ordained today. As we learned in the chapter on Confirmation, the laying on of hands is an ancient symbol of passing on a spiritual gift. The laying on of hands and the words of the ordination prayer are the **sign of Holy Orders**. The words of the ordination prayer tell us that this gift is a share in the priesthood of Christ. It asks God to:

. . . give these servants of yours the dignity of the presbyterate [priesthood]. Renew the Spirit of holiness within them. By your divine gift may they attain the second order in the hierarchy and exemplify right conduct in their lives.

We learn from this prayer that God increases his Spirit in these men, giving them the special powers of the priesthood. The life of God is increased within them, and they receive all the graces they need to become good, holy priests. Like Baptism and Confirmation, Holy Orders puts a sacramental seal (spiritual mark) on the soul. This shows God that they have been united to Jesus, our High Priest.

A Wonderful Calling

The call of God to the priesthood is very wonderful. It is one of the greatest honors which a man can receive in this life. We should pray for our parish priests every day and also ask Jesus to send the Church more good, holy servants.

We should always show respect to our priests and realize that their lives are very hard. They spend all their days celebrating Mass, hearing confessions, counseling people, and attending to the needs of a busy parish. But their life, if it is lived in faith, hope, and love for God will surely lead to everlasting happiness! The holy Father of the Church, Saint Basil the Great once said: "The ministry of the priesthood is a great work which will bring you to the Kingdom of Heaven."

Words to Know:
> apostolic succession
> priesthood of the faithful
> ordained priesthood   hierarchy
> bishops   priest   deacon
> sign of Holy Orders

Q. 225 *What is the Sacrament of Holy Orders?*
Holy Orders is the sacrament by which a man is configured to Christ and is given the power to continue the apostolic ministry as a bishop, priest, or deacon (CCC 1536).

Q. 226 *Who confers the Sacrament of Holy Orders?*
The bishop confers the Sacrament of Holy Orders (CCC 1576).

Q. 227 *What are the degrees of the Sacrament of Holy Orders?*
The degrees of the Sacrament of Holy Orders are bishop, priest, and deacon (CCC 1554).

Q. 228 *How does the bishop confer the Sacrament of Holy Orders?*
The bishop confers the Sacrament of Holy Orders by imposing hands and praying that the Holy Spirit be sent upon the man receiving Holy Orders (CCC 1573, 1576).

Q. 229 *What is a bishop?*

A bishop is a man who has received the fullness of the Sacrament of Holy Orders, which includes the power to confer the Sacrament of Holy Orders on others, and to teach, sanctify, and govern the people of a diocese (CCC 1558, 1594).

Q. 230 *What is a priest?*

A priest is a man who has received, through the Sacrament of Holy Orders, a share in the apostolic ministry, including the power to consecrate the Holy Eucharist and to forgive sins.

Q. 231 *What is a deacon?*

A deacon is a man who, through the Sacrament of Holy Orders, is ordained to assist the bishop and priests in service to the Church (CCC 1596).

Q. 232 *How does a man go about entering into Holy Orders?*

A man goes about entering into Holy Orders by discerning a vocation, or call from God, and submitting his discernment to the judgment of the Church (CCC 1578).

CHAPTER 29

The Sacrament of Matrimony

As the church is subject to Christ, so let wives also be subject in everything to their husbands. Husbands, love your wives, as Christ loved the church and gave himself up for her.

Ephesians 5:24–25

In this chapter we are going to look at the second sacrament of service, Matrimony. Marriage is the oldest form of community among

man. It was given to us by God right after he created the first man:

> Then the LORD God said, "It is not good that the man should be alone; I will make him a helper fit for him." So out of the ground the LORD God formed every beast of the field and every bird of the air, and brought them to the man to see what he would call them; and whatever the man called every living creature, that was its name. The man gave names to all cattle, and to the birds of the air, and to every beast of the field; but for the man there was not found a helper fit for him. So the LORD God caused a deep sleep to fall upon the man, and while he slept took one of his ribs and closed up its place with flesh; and the rib which the LORD God had taken from the man he made into a woman and brought her to the man. Then the man said, "This at last is bone of my bones and flesh of my flesh; she shall be called Woman, because she was taken out of Man." Therefore a man leaves his father and his mother and

cleaves to his wife, and they become one flesh. And the man and his wife were both naked, and were not ashamed (Gen 2:18–25).

After having joined Adam and Eve as husband and wife, God said to them: "Be fruitful and multiply, and fill the earth and subdue it" (Gen 1:28).

The Purpose of Marriage

From these two passages from Genesis and from the teachings of Christ and his Church we learn that there are two special purposes of marriage.

God gave the man and wife to each other as partners. By their love for each other they support one another in life. They help each other to know, love, and serve God on earth so that they will live with him in heaven. This partnership is often called *mutual love*.

The other purpose of marriage is the bearing and bringing up of children in a loving family. Through the holy gift of their bodies to one another, husband and wife cooperate with God in bringing new human life into the world. This second purpose is often called **procreation**. The marriage commitment of the man and woman makes sure that the children will have a home and family to grow up in. It protects the little ones and provides for their true development as children of God.

The Sacrament of Matrimony

Even before Jesus made marriage a sacrament, it was seen as a life-long union of husband and wife, in which they promised to love each other and live with one another until death. Of course, we human beings do not always go along with God's plan. Our weak human nature sometimes destroys his plan for marriage by such things as divorce and adultery. But this does not change the purpose of Matrimony as our Creator meant it to be.

One day, some leaders of the Jews asked Jesus what his teaching on marriage was. He answered them, saying:

> He answered, "Have you not read that he who made them from the beginning made them male and female, and said, 'For this reason a man shall leave his father and mother and be joined to his wife, and the two shall become one'? So they are no longer two but one. What therefore God has joined together, let not man put asunder." They said to him, "Why then did Moses command one to give a certificate of divorce, and to put her away?" He said to them, "For your hardness of heart Moses allowed you to divorce your wives, but from the beginning it was not so. And I say to you: whoever divorces his wife, except for unchastity, and marries another, commits adultery" (Mt 19:4–9).

At the beginning of Jesus' public life, he attended a wedding feast and worked his first miracle there. He did this in order to bless the marriage with his presence. He made marriage a sacrament and a symbol of the love he has for his body the Church. Just as Jesus will always love his Church and never leave her, so the husband must always love his wife and stay with her until death.

What is Christian Marriage?

In order for a couple to have a sacramental Christian marriage, both of them must be baptized. They must intend to live their marriage according to God's plan, which means a *life-long* relationship and openness to whatever children God may send them. On their wedding day they agree to remain with one another through good times and bad, in riches or in poverty, in sickness or in health.

To help couples live a good Christian marriage the Church has made some laws concerning the celebration of this sacrament. If a man and woman do not agree to marry according to these rules or with respect for God's plan, then they have an **invalid marriage**. This means that a true union never took place, and they are single people in the eyes of God.

The Rite of Matrimony

The wedding rite, or ceremony, usually takes place during Mass, but this is not required for the celebration of the sacrament. Also, the priest or deacon is not the one who administers the sacrament to the couple. He is there to witness it for the Church and to bless it in God's name. The man and wife are the ones who give the sacrament to each other by the words of the solemn **wedding promises**.

After the homily at Mass, the priest asks the couple if they have come to the wedding freely, without anyone or anything pressuring them to do so. He then asks if they agree to live their marriage according to God's plan. If they can truly say "yes," then the ceremony continues.

The bride and groom join hands and pronounce the vows to one another. This is the **sign of Matrimony**. As you know, a vow is your solemn promise to do what you say. To break it would be a mortal sin. The wedding vows are usually worded like this:

I, (name), take you, (name), to be my wife (husband). I promise to be true to you in good times and in bad, in sickness and in health. I will love you and honor you all the days of my life (Rite of Matrimony).

After this, the newlyweds usually give rings to one another. The priest blesses these rings so that they may be signs of their love and fidelity.

The Mass continues as usual until before Holy Communion when the Nuptial (Wedding) Blessing is given. This is a special blessing which only two Christians may receive. It asks God to make their life holy, to keep them faithful to one another, to send them the gift of children, and to bring them to heaven when they die. At the end of the Mass another blessing is given and the ceremony ends.

Through this sacrament God makes the two people *one flesh*. This means that they cannot be separated in his eyes, any more than a human body can be separated and still live. God also gives them all of the graces they will need to be faithful to each other and to be good parents. He calls them to be witnesses for Jesus and the Christian life among their relatives and friends and in the world around them.

Modern Day Attacks on Marriage

As we discussed earlier in this lesson, many people today do not think of marriage according to God's plan. This is because the world has different values from those of Christ. It attacks the Sacrament of Matrimony in many ways. How? By approving of divorce and adultery, by worshipping money and possessions as false gods in society, by teaching young people that sex outside of marriage and other unchaste acts are acceptable; by encouraging a negative attitude toward large families, and by encouraging the use of contraceptives and permitting abortions.

Every Christian couple—married or engaged—must be aware of these false values. They should try to understand God's true plan for marriage by studying the teachings of the Church. Daily prayer together will help them to be strong as they try to live out their lifelong vows. Young people can prepare themselves for marriage by asking God to send them good Christian friends. In this way they will not be tempted to marry just anyone, but only someone who really loves them and who loves God. It is never too early to prepare yourself for this holy and wonderful sacrament!

Words to Know:

procreation   sign of Matrimony
invalid marriage   wedding promises

Q. 233 *What is the Sacrament of Matrimony?*

In the Sacrament of Matrimony, a baptized man and a baptized woman are united in Christ for the good of one another and for the procreation and education of children (CCC 1601).

Q. 234 *Who is the minister of the Sacrament of Matrimony?*

The spouses, by conferring the Sacrament of Matrimony on each other, are the ministers of this sacrament (CCC 1623).

Q. 235 *What duties do the spouses assume?*

The spouses assume the duties of living together in a holy way, helping each other with unfailing affection in their temporal and spiritual necessities, and raising their children in the Catholic faith (CCC 1638, 1641).

CHAPTER 30

Sacramentals

Now there are varieties of gifts, but the same Spirit; and there are varieties of service, but the same Lord; and there are varieties of working, but it is the same God who inspires them all in every one.

1 Corinthians 12:4–6

So far, we have considered the seven sacraments of the Church. As we have seen, the sacraments are sacred signs given by Jesus to communicate to us his life of grace. But there are other sacred signs in the Church in addition to the sacraments. These are *like* the sacraments, which is why they are called sacramentals. A **sacramental** is a sacred sign. Unlike the seven sacraments, sacramentals were not instituted by Jesus himself. They were established by the Church. They prepare us to receive grace, especially through the sacraments. Sacramentals bring their blessings through the prayers of the Church, rather than through the promise of Jesus. They help bless and make holy many situations in a Christian's life.

The sacramentals are different from the sacraments in important ways. The Church instituted the sacramentals; Christ instituted the sacraments. Also, the sacramentals do not give us grace in the way that the sacraments do. The sacraments give us grace by the power and promise of Jesus Christ, provided we are properly disposed to receive them. The sacramentals, on the other hand, help us to be ready to

receive grace and cooperate with it. They give us grace by the prayer of the Church and our own cooperation.

Blessings are important sacramentals. They praise God for his goodness and ask for his gifts to be bestowed on us. At the end of Holy Mass, the priest bestows a blessing on the people in the name of the Holy Trinity.

Some blessings consecrate or dedicate persons to God. For example, there are blessings for those making religious professions or those entering into non-ordained ministries in the Church such as readers at Mass. Other blessings consecrate, or dedicate, objects or places to God. For example, objects such as altars, holy oils, rosaries, medals, sacred vessels, and vestments are blessed. Church buildings are places that are blessed. Perhaps the most common blessing is the blessing of meals.

Popular Piety

The sacraments and the sacramentals are very important. But there are other ways we grow in our Catholic faith. Popular piety is one of these ways. **Piety** is reverence or devotion to God or the saints. Popular piety is the way people express their personal reverence or devotion to God or the saints, in addition to the ceremonies of the Sacred Liturgy. Popular piety includes things such as veneration of relics, pilgrimages to holy places, processions, the Stations of the Cross, and praying the Rosary.

Sometimes different cultures have their own forms of popular piety. For example, some cultures have devotion to a particular saint. In America, many people have special devotion to Our Lady of Guadalupe. This is because the Blessed Mother appeared to Saint Juan Diego in Mexico, which is part of North America. The Church is made up of many different cultures. This diversity of cultures allows the Church to share and express her faith in many different ways. In this way, the Church shows that she is truly Catholic—universal.

The Church is always careful to make sure that popular devotions and practices are truly Catholic. But even when the Church approves a form of popular piety, the sacraments are still more important. Popular piety should help us grow closer to God by helping us to receive the sacraments more deeply.

Words to Know:

sacramental   piety

Grace Before Meals

Bless us, O Lord and these, thy gifts, which we are about to receive, from thy bounty, through Christ, our Lord. *Amen.* We give thee thanks for all thy benefits and may the souls of the faithful departed, through the mercy of God, rest in peace. *Amen.*

Q. 236 *What is a sacramental?*

A sacramental is a sacred sign that prepares people to receive grace, especially through the sacraments (CCC 1677).

Q. 237 *What is popular piety?*

Popular piety refers to the way people express their personal reverence or devotion to God or the saints, in addition to the ceremonies of the Sacred Liturgy (CCC 1674).

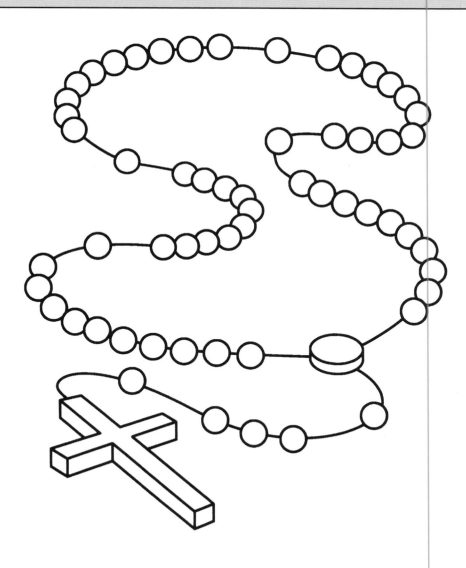

CHAPTER 31

Mary, Mediatrix of Grace

And the angel said to her, "Do not be afraid, Mary, for you have found favor with God."

Luke 1:30

As Jesus hung upon the wood of the Cross, he gave us one of the most beautiful gifts in the Church—Mary as our Blessed Mother. From the Cross he said to her, "Woman, behold, your son." He was talking about the Apostle John, who stood by the Cross with Mary. Then he said to John, "Behold, your mother" (Jn 19:26–27).

These words of Jesus were not meant for John alone, but for every one of his followers. The young apostle was the only disciple to be with Jesus until the end. He represents each one of us who could not be there in person.

Love for Mary has always been a sign of true Christianity. All of the saints have loved her more than anyone, except for God, of course. Why? Because she was so greatly loved by God, who chose her to be the Mother of his Son. Saint Gregory the Great, a Pope of the sixth century, revealed the early Church's devotion to Mary in these words: "If anyone does not love the Holy Mother of God, he is far from God."

Mary's Role in Our Salvation

Mary's birth was an event of great joy for the world because it meant that the Savior was soon to arrive! Every year, on September 8, the Church celebrates her birthday with this prayer:

Your birth, O Virgin Mother of God, proclaims joy to the world, for from you arose the glorious Sun of Justice, Christ Our Lord (Liturgy of the Hours).

These words remind us of Mary's role in our salvation. She was to make it possible for Jesus to come among us as a man. Through her cooperation with God's plan we were saved by the life, death, and Resurrection of her Son.

She conceived Jesus and gave birth to the Savior in Bethlehem. But that was not the end of her work for us. As Jesus grew and began preaching the good news of salvation, Mary continued to devote herself to him. She listened to his teachings and put them into practice. She became the perfect disciple of Jesus and gave us an example to follow.

Mary looked after the needs of Jesus, and she does the same thing for us today, as she looks down upon us from heaven. She prays for us and asks Jesus to give us all that we need. Sometimes the Virgin Mary is called the channel (or **Mediatrix**) of all grace. This is because she is the Mother of Jesus, and without Jesus we would have no grace. Since Jesus has come to us by being conceived and born of Mary, we can say that all grace comes through her. Pope Pius XI (d. 1939) summed up this teaching in a few simple words: "Everything comes to us from Almighty God through the hands of Our Lady."

When the sad events of Jesus' suffering and death occurred, faithful Mary refused to abandon him. She courageously stood near him as he hung upon the Cross, offering her sorrow to the Father. She united her heart with Jesus' in asking God to accept his death for the forgiveness of our sins.

After the Ascension of Jesus into heaven, Mary stayed with the apostles as they prayed for the gift of the Holy Spirit. From then until she went to heaven, Our Lady was a loving mother to the members of the Church. She reminded them about Jesus and told them stories from his childhood. Some of these are recorded for us in the Gospels of Saint Matthew and Saint Luke. We call Mary the **Mother of the Church**. Just as she was the mother of Christ's human body, so now she is the Mother of his spiritual body, the Church.

Mary truly was full of grace. As a sign of God's special love for her he bestowed on her special privileges. Mary is the only human besides Jesus who was always free from original sin. Mary was conceived without the stain of original sin; we call this her Immaculate Conception. This means that from the moment of Mary's conception in her mother's womb she was full of God's grace. God gave her this special gift because she was to be the mother of God's son, Jesus Christ. Mary's perpetual virginity is another privilege God bestowed on her. Only Mary can claim the title of Mother and Virgin. We celebrate the feast of the Assumption, another of Mary's privileges, in which she was taken up into heaven body and soul. The Church maintains that since Mary was free from sin she would also be preserved from the consequences of sin. Finally, Mary has been given the exalted title of Mother of God since she truly is the mother of Jesus, who is God.

Let Mary Be Your Mother

Jesus never forced anyone to become a Christian. He wanted people to choose freely to follow him. In the same way, Mary never forces us to live as her children. She wants us freely to ask her to take care of us.

There is a special way to ask Our Lady to be our Mother. It is called **Total Consecration to Mary**. This means that we give ourselves—body and soul, all that we have and are—to her. We do this so that she can use these things to make us like Jesus. This consecration was used by many saints, especially Saint Louis De Montfort (18th century) and Saint Maximilian Kolbe (d. 1941). They said that it is the easiest way to become a good Christian and a saint. If you want Mary to be your Mother, consecrate yourself to her every day by using this simple prayer:

Accept me, O Mary, as your own child, and take charge of my salvation (Saint Alphonsus Liguori, d. 1787).

Words to Know:
Mediatrix   Mother of the Church
Total Consecration to Mary

We believe that the Blessed Mother of God, the New Eve, Mother of the Church, continues in heaven her maternal role with regard to Christ's members, cooperating with the birth and growth of divine life in the souls of the redeemed.

—Credo of the People of God

Q. 238 *What is the Immaculate Conception?*

The Immaculate Conception is the gift of God by which Mary was preserved from original sin, from the moment of her conception, by the merits of Jesus Christ (CCC 491).

Q. 239 *What is the Assumption of Mary?*

The Assumption of Mary is a gift from God, given to Mary at the end of her earthly life, whereby she was taken up into heaven body and soul (CCC 966).

Q. 240 *Why is it proper to say that Mary is the Mother of God?*

It is proper to say that Mary is the Mother of God because she is the mother of Jesus Christ, the Second Person of the Holy Trinity, who is true God and True Man (CCC 495).

Appendix

WORDS TO KNOW

ABSOLUTION: The act or prayer by which the priest, in the name of Christ and by the authority of the Church, forgives our sins. It is one of the signs of the Sacrament of Penance.

ACT OF CONTRITION: A prayer in which we tell God that we are sorry for our sins.

ACTUAL GRACE: Supernatural help from God in which he inspires us to do good and avoid evil. The desire to pray and to help others are examples of actual graces.

ALTAR: A table which has been specially dedicated to God for the offering of sacrifices. Holy Mass is usually offered on an altar.

ANOINT (ANOINTING): The act of pouring oil on someone or something in a religious ceremony. In Christianity it is a sign of being specially chosen by God to share in Jesus' triple office of priest, prophet, and king.

APOSTOLIC SUCCESSION: The unbroken chain of bishops from the apostles to the present day. The apostles received the power to become bishops and priests from Jesus himself. They, in turn, passed this power on to others through Holy Orders. This *passing on* of Holy Orders down to our own day is called apostolic succession. Only the Catholic and Orthodox Churches have this succession. Only their clergy thus share in the Sacrament of Holy Orders.

ARIANISM: The heresy which denied the truth that Jesus is God, the second Person of the Holy Trinity.

ARK OF THE COVENANT: The special chest in which the Jews placed the tablets of the Ten Commandments. It was very sacred to God's people who carried it with them during their journey to the Promised Land. It was a prefigurement of the tabernacle in which the Body of Christ is kept in Catholic churches today.

BAPTISMAL SEAL: The permanent spiritual (invisible) mark, or sign, on the soul of the baptized that shows we belong to Christ. It can never be removed, not even by the most terrible of sins.

BAPTISM OF BLOOD: The possibility of salvation for those who have not received the Sacrament of Baptism but who have died as martyrs for Christ.

BAPTISM OF DESIRE: The possibility of salvation for those who, through no fault of their own, do not know about the necessity of the Sacrament of Baptism in order to enter heaven.

BEATITUDES: The promises of true happiness (beatitude = state of blessedness or spiritual happiness) that Jesus made to those who follow his teachings. The traditional beatitudes can be found in the Sermon on the Mount (Mt 5:3–11).

BENEDICTION: A Eucharistic devotion of Roman Rite Catholics. It consists of hymns, readings from the Bible, and the blessing of the people with the Holy Eucharist. It is a way of worshipping God and affirming our belief in the Real Presence of Jesus in the Blessed Sacrament.

BISHOPS: Successors of the apostles who have received the fullness of the priesthood. Bishops are the spiritual leaders of Christians in their dioceses (geographical areas). They alone can ordain men to the priesthood and to the office of bishop. United with the Pope, they are the official teachers of the faith in the world.

BODY: The physical part of man that is given life by the soul. The body is created by God, and it is thus a good and holy thing. At the end of the world, the body will rise from the dead and be reunited with the soul.

BYZANTINE CATHOLICS: Those members of the Catholic Church whose ways of worshipping and living the faith come from the ancient traditions of Byzantium (the Eastern part of the ancient Roman Empire). In the early Church both Rome and Byzantium were important centers of Christianity. Each developed its own way of expressing the one true faith in worship and customs. Byzantine Catholics are the second largest group in the Church, Roman Catholics being the first.

CARDINAL VIRTUES: The four main virtues or habits of good actions. They are prudence, justice, temperance, and fortitude.

CATHOLIC FAITH: The religion which began with Christ and the Twelve Apostles almost two thousand years ago. It is the one true faith for it comes to us from God himself, who became man and taught us the true way of worshipping and believing. The special sign of the Catholic faith is the members' obedience to the Pope.

CHANGE OF HEART: The firm decision to love God and our neighbors more than ourselves. This means that we do our best to give up sin, to pray more, and to do good to others. It is sometimes called *conversion*.

CHARITY: The supernatural power we receive from God that helps us to love him and our neighbor more than ourselves. It is often called *love*. Love for God means that we obey his Commandments and the teachings of Christ. Love for neighbor means that we want only what is good for others and that we seek the good of all men.

COMMUNION OF SAINTS: The relationship that exists between all of the members of the Church, whether they are in heaven, in purgatory, or on earth. Those in heaven pray for us and help us in our needs. They also pray for those in purgatory. The souls in purgatory pray for us too. We can help them by our own prayers on their behalf. Belief in the Communion of Saints is quite ancient in the Church, going back to the times of the apostles. The word *saint* here means anyone who is in the state of sanctifying grace.

CONFESSIONAL: The place where the Sacrament of Penance is normally celebrated. Sometimes it is called a reconciliation room or chapel.

CONFESSION OF SINS: The telling of one's sins to a priest in order to receive absolution. It can also mean the telling of one's sins privately to God. For example, in the penitential rite of the Mass we privately confess our sins to God, but this is not a way of receiving the Sacrament of Penance.

CONSCIENCE: The ability we have to judge right from wrong according to what we have learned from faith and reason. For a person to have a *good conscience*, he must study the Bible and the teachings of the Church and put them into practice.

CONSECRATED: Someone or something that is specially blessed and set aside for God. Every Christian is consecrated by Baptism. Altars and churches are consecrated in special ceremonies. We must treat consecrated people or things with great respect and reverence for they are dear to God.

COVENANT: In the Old Testament a covenant is the agreement made between God and the people of Israel (Jews). God promised to love and protect his people. In return they agreed to be loyal to him. In the New Testament, the *new and everlasting* covenant was made between God and men by Jesus Christ. God promises to free us from our sins and bring us to heaven. In return, we agree to give up our sins, be baptized, and follow the teachings of Christ and the Church. Every Holy Mass renews this covenant and the words of Consecration tell us that it is a covenant made by the Blood of Christ.

CREATE: To create means to make something from nothing. When God created the universe, he made it from nothing. God is all powerful and the source of all that is.

CREED: Creed comes from the Latin word *credo*, "I believe." It is a statement of our beliefs as Christians (such as the Apostles' Creed or the Nicene Creed).

DEACON: A man who is specially ordained and shares in the sacrament of orders. He serves the Church by his sacred ministry, for example, at Mass, by preaching, as ordinary minister of Baptism and Communion, as official witness of the Church at weddings, as well as by performing works of mercy for the needy. Deacons may be *transitional* (studying to become priests) or *permanent* (who are called to the vocation of deacon for life).

DIVINE REVELATION: The truths that we have learned from God himself about religion, mankind, and the world. Divine revelation was a free gift from God to us. Without it we would never have known about such things as the Trinity, the Incarnation, or other important truths. Divine revelation began with Adam and Eve; it came to an end with the death of Saint John the Evangelist (about A.D. 100).

DOCETISM: The heresy which denied the truth that the Son of God became a real man, Jesus Christ. Docetists believed that the human body was evil. Therefore, God would not have become man.

ECUMENICAL COUNCIL: The gathering of all the world's bishops together with the Pope for a special reason. The councils are named after the cities or churches in which they have taken place. The very first council was that of Jerusalem, about A.D. 49. The latest was Vatican II, 1962–1965.

EUCHARISTIC FAST: Refraining from food or drink (except water and medicine) for one hour before receiving Holy Communion. (However, the sick or the elderly and those who care for them may receive the Eucharist without fasting.) We happily offer Jesus this small sacrifice as a way of showing special respect for the Holy Eucharist, our spiritual food and drink.

EVANGELISTS: The title given to the four authors of the Gospels: Saints Matthew, Mark, Luke, and John. It comes from the Latin word *evangelium*, which means "good news" or "gospel."

EXAMINATION OF CONSCIENCE: The time we spend in thinking about our sins in order to do better in the future. The examination of conscience is an important way to have a change of heart and to prepare for the sacrament of Penance.

EXODUS: The name given to the journey of the Jews from Egypt to the Promised Land. It is also the name of the second book of the Old Testament, which tells us about this journey.

EXORCISM: The special and powerful ceremony of the Church by which the devil, or his evil influence, is driven away from a person. All Catholics are exorcised at Baptism.

FAITH: The supernatural power that we receive from God which helps us to believe in all that he has revealed through the Bible, Jesus, and the Church. Faith is necessary for salvation.

FALLEN ANGELS: Those angels who refused to serve God and do his will. They were created good by the Lord but became evil by their own choice. Led by Lucifer (Satan), they tempt us to sin and try to lead us away from God.

FORERUNNER: In ancient times this was someone who announced the arrival of an important person. While the noble visitor was traveling to a town, the forerunner would run ahead of the person in order to prepare the people for his visit. The Church gives this title to Saint John the Baptist since it was his duty to prepare the people for Jesus' mission.

FORTITUDE: Fortitude is one of the cardinal virtues. It means strength and determination in loving God and one's neighbor.

GIFT OF FAITH: The free gift that God gives to us so that we might believe in Jesus and his Gospel. Without this gift we would never be able to know what is necessary for salvation.

GOOD ANGELS: Those angels who loved God and were ever ready to do his will. The good angels are led by Saint Michael the Archangel. They help us to know, love, and serve God so that we can go to live with him forever in heaven. Everyone has a Guardian Angel who is specially assigned to him during life.

GOOD NEWS: Another word for gospel. The gospel is the good news that we are freed from sin and able to enter heaven. This has been accomplished for us by Jesus' death and Resurrection. The gospel is also good news because it reveals the truth to us. Jesus'

teachings in the four Gospels show us how to live if we want to reach heaven. This is why the Gospel is read at every Holy Mass.

GOSPELS: The four accounts or records we have about the life, death, and Resurrection of Jesus. They tell us what Christ did and said while he lived on earth.

GRACE: The free gift that God gives us by which he helps us to reach heaven. There are different kinds of graces: sanctifying, sacramental, and actual.

HEAVEN: The place and condition of perfect happiness with God forever. Heaven is for those who have died in God's love, i.e., in the state of grace.

HELL: The place and condition of never-ending separation from God. Hell is for those who have died in the state of serious sin.

HERALD: Someone whose duty it is to announce the coming of an important royal person. The Church gives this title to Saint John the Baptist. He had the mission of announcing the coming of Christ our King.

HERESIES: Religious beliefs that corrupt the true teachings of Christ and the Church. Those who teach or believe these false ideas are called *heretics*.

HIERARCHY: The order of authority in the Church. The bishops united under the Pope as the true successors of Saint Peter and the apostles form the *hierarchy* in the Church. It is their duty to teach the faith, govern Christians in their dioceses, and administer the sacraments.

HOLY BIBLE: The collection of books which the Church teaches to be inspired by God. There are seventy-three books in the Holy Bible, which is divided into two sections: the Old Testament and the New Testament. The purpose of these writings is to teach us the truth about God and salvation. The Bible is also called *Sacred Scripture*.

HOPE: The supernatural power we receive that helps us to trust in God. Hope gives us confidence that God will forgive our sins and bring us to heaven.

HOSTS: The round wafers of bread used at Mass. At the Consecration they are changed into Jesus Christ, the Bread of Life.

HUMAN REASON: The power which human beings have by which we are able to think and grow in our understanding of the truth. Human reason can help us to learn many things about God. But it cannot tell us everything there is to know about him.

HYPOSTATIC UNION: This is the mystery that in Christ the divine and human natures are united in the second Person of the Holy Trinity.

IDOL: Any creature (created thing) that we honor and worship as a god. Idols can be people (such as sports heroes or movie stars) or things (such as money or fashionable clothing). Something becomes an idol when we desire it and honor it more than God. Idols are also called false *gods* in the Bible (such as in the First Commandment).

IMMORTAL: To be free from death. The soul of every human being is immortal, that is, it will never die. When death comes to the body, the soul lives on in heaven, purgatory, or hell.

INCARNATION: The truth that God became man. The Incarnation refers to the conception and birth of Jesus, the Son of God become man through Mary.

INDEFECTIBILITY: The truth that the Catholic Church will last until the end of the world. It will always teach and shepherd Christians in Jesus' name. Nothing will be able to destroy it.

INDULGENCE: The taking away of the punishment our sins deserve. We can do this on earth through prayer, penance, and good works, or we can make up for our sins in purgatory.

INDWELLING: The truth that the Holy Trinity lives in our souls by sanctifying grace. This makes our bodies temples of God.

INFALLIBILITY: The truth that the Catholic Church, by the special help of the Holy Spirit, is kept free from any error in teaching us about what we must believe (faith) and how we must live (morals). Only the Pope, or all the bishops united under the Pope, can teach us *infallibly*.

INSPIRATION: The special help which God gave to the men who wrote the books of the Bible. Inspiration means that these men were guided by the Holy Spirit so that they wrote down *only* those truths that God wanted them to write. This is why we call the Bible the *inspired* word of God.

INVALID MARRIAGE: A marriage that in the eyes of God really never took place because something important was missing from it. For example, if the man and woman did not intend to be married according to God's plan (life-long mutual love, procreation) then they may be in an *invalid* marriage.

ISRAEL: The name first given by God to Jacob, the son of Isaac. It later became a name for God's People in the Old Testament. Today, it is the name of the Jewish nation-state in the Mideast. Sometimes, the Catholic Church is called the *new Israel* to remind us that Jesus gathered God's People into a New Testament community.

JUSTICE: One of the cardinal virtues. A just person is one who renders to another what is rightfully his. Justice moves us to respect the rights and dignity of all human beings.

KINGDOM OF GOD: In the Gospels, the Kingdom of God means both heaven and the Church. It is also called the Kingdom of Heaven and the Reign of God. People belong to this spiritual Kingdom by faith in Jesus Christ and the reception of Baptism.

LAW: Another name for the Ten Commandments of God. In Christian vocabulary it also includes the New Testament commandments of Christ.

MAGISTERIUM: The teaching office or authority in the Church. The magisterium is exercised by the Pope and the bishops united with him. By Christ's command, all Christians are solemnly obliged to obey the teachings of the magisterium.

MARKS OF THE CHURCH: The four special signs that point out the true Church of Jesus Christ. These four marks are found in the Nicene Creed as *one, holy, catholic, and apostolic*. Only in the Catholic Church can all four of these marks be found.

MEDIATOR: Someone who is a "go-between" for others. Jesus Christ is the one true mediator between God and mankind. As mediator he prays for us and asks the Father to forgive our sins.

MEDIATRIX: A title for the Blessed Virgin Mary. It reminds us that Jesus came to us through her and that she now prays for us to Jesus her Son.

MERCY: The loving-kindness that God has for mankind. Because God is *merciful* he forgives us our sins and brings us to heaven. Christ commands each one of us to be merciful to others, forgiving them whatever wrongs they have done to us.

MESSIAH: The Hebrew word *Messiah* is translated as *Christ* in the Greek language and means "the anointed one." Thus we call Our Lord: Jesus *Christ* (Jesus the Messiah). The word *Messiah* was first used by the Jews to refer to the savior promised to Adam and Eve. Waiting for the Messiah's coming was an important part of Judaism. (Some Jews of today are still waiting for the Messiah to come. They do not believe that Jesus was the Anointed One. The Bible and Tradition assure us that he was.)

MIRACLES: Events that are far above the natural powers of either man or nature. They are supernatural happenings, done by God in order to prove some truth (such as Christ's teachings) or to show the holiness of someone (such as a saint). Sometimes an extraordinary event can be worked by the devil in order to fool Christians and to lead us away from God. It is important that we listen to the decisions of the Church before we believe in any modern-day miracles.

MONSTRANCE: The sacred vessel in which the consecrated Host is placed for exposition or Benediction of the Blessed Sacrament.

MORTAL SIN: A serious offense against the law of God, which destroys the life of grace in our souls. For a sin to be *mortal* three conditions must be present: 1) the action must be seriously wrong, 2) we must *know* that it is seriously wrong, and 3) and we must do it *freely*, that is, without anyone or anything forcing us to do it. Even *one* mortal sin can bring us to hell. Thus it is important to confess such sins as soon as possible and to avoid whatever leads us to commit these sins.

MOTHER OF THE CHURCH: A title of the Blessed Virgin Mary. It reminds us that she is the Mother of Jesus who is head of the Church. It also tells us that she is *our* Mother, for we are all members of the Church.

MUTUAL LOVE: One of the two purposes of marriage. Mutual love means that both husband and wife will love each other more than anyone else (except God). They vow to do this until death. Love does not mean that we always *feel good* about someone, but that we will honor, respect, and care for him.

MYSTERY: In religious vocabulary the word "mystery" means a truth that our limited human minds will never be able to understand fully. Some mysteries of our faith are the Trinity, the Hypostatic Union, the Incarnation, the Resurrection of Jesus, and the Holy Eucharist.

MYSTERY OF FAITH: This term refers to the Holy Eucharist which is the Sacrifice of Jesus. We still use this title at every Holy Mass. Immediately after the Consecration, the priest says: "Let us proclaim the Mystery of Faith." We then reaffirm our belief in the death and Resurrection of the Lord, which the Mass re-enacts for us.

MYSTICAL BODY OF CHRIST: A name for the Church. It reminds us that we are all united to Jesus and to one another just as the various parts of the human body are united to form one person. This way of looking at the Church reminds us that we are a close community of believers and that everyone must do his part in bringing Jesus and the gospel to the world.

NATIVITY: Another word for human birth. The Church celebrates the nativity of Jesus (Christmas) on December 25. We also celebrate the nativities, or birthdays, of Our Lady (September 8) and of Saint John the Baptist (June 24).

NEW TESTAMENT: The second section of the Holy Bible. Made up of only twenty-seven books, it is the most important part of the Scriptures because it tells us about the life, teachings, death, and Resurrection of Jesus Christ.

NICENE CREED: The *Profession of Faith* which we say at every Sunday Mass. Dating from the year A.D. 381, it contains the major beliefs of Christians. Along with the more

ancient *Apostles' Creed*, it is a very important prayer for Christians.

OCCASION OF SIN: Any person, place, or thing that can lead us to disobey the holy law of God. An occasion of sin may be different for each person. We can know what persons, places, or things lead us to sin by examining our consciences daily.

OIL OF THE CATECHUMENS: Oil which is blessed by a bishop for use in the sacraments of Baptism and Holy Orders.

OIL OF THE SICK: Oil which is blessed by a bishop for use in the sacrament of Anointing. Oil is a symbol of strength and healing.

OLD TESTAMENT: The first section of the Holy Bible. It is made up of forty-six books which tell us about the history and religious beliefs of the Jewish people. The main theme of the Old Testament is the coming of the Messiah.

ORDAINED PRIESTHOOD: The priesthood which is given to a Catholic man through the sacrament of Holy Orders. While *all* Christians share in the priesthood of Christ, *ordained* priests, like Jesus, offer the Sacrifice of the Mass and forgive sins. Priests are often assigned to a *parish* where they are in charge of our spiritual well-being.

ORDERS: The sacrament that, by the imposition of the bishop's hands confers on a man the grace and spiritual power to sanctify others. There are three forms of this sacrament, also called sacramental orders: namely, diaconate (deacons), priesthood (priests), and episcopate (bishops). Although there are three forms, there is only one sacrament of orders.

ORIGINAL SIN: The very first sin to be committed by man. It was committed by Adam with his wife Eve, the parents of the human race. Because of original sin, mankind was separated from God and denied entrance into heaven. Jesus came to restore mankind to friendship with God. By his death and Resurrection he reunited us with the Father and restored the life of grace to our souls.

PARABLE: A short story that is meant to teach a religious lesson. Jesus used parables in teaching the people about God and salvation.

PARACLETE: A title for the Holy Spirit. It means someone who pleads before a judge on behalf of someone else. Jesus himself used this title in speaking about the Holy Spirit. Saint Paul the Apostle said that the Spirit would plead for us before God, and help us to pray.

PASCHAL MYSTERY: This term comes from the Hebrew word for "Passover," a feast Jews celebrated in remembrance of their liberation from Egypt. The Last Supper was a Passover meal Jesus celebrated with his apostles. So "paschal mystery" refers to the suffering, death, and Resurrection of Jesus by which we are saved from our sins.

PASSOVER: The ancient Jewish ceremonial supper which recalls the Exodus from Egypt. Passover commemorates the deliverance of the Jewish people from death by the blood of the lamb that was sprinkled over their doors in Egypt.

PATRIARCH: A title given to the founding fathers of the Jewish people in the Old Testament. There are four Old Testament patriarchs: Abraham, Isaac, Jacob, and Joseph.

PATRON SAINTS: The saints after whom we are named at Baptism and at Confirmation. These saints pray for us in a special way and help us to reach heaven. We should learn about our patron saints and try to love God as they did.

PENANCE: The practice of self-denial by such acts as fasting, giving money to the poor, and spending extra time in prayer. The purpose of penance is to help us have a *change of heart* so that we may grow in love for God and our neighbors.

PENTECOST: The special feast of the Holy Spirit. It recalls the coming of the Spirit upon the apostles. We celebrate Pentecost fifty days after Easter.

PEOPLE OF GOD: A title for the Church. It reminds us that the Church is a visible community of people who are chosen by God to be his own. All baptized Christians belong to the People of God.

PIETY: Reverence to God and the saints. Piety also refers to religious expression in devotions and prayers.

PILGRIM CHURCH: Another title for the Church. It reminds us that we are *pilgrims*, that is, people who are on a spiritual journey to the Kingdom of God. It reminds us that life on earth is only a temporary thing, and that heaven is our true home.

POPE: The visible leader of the Church and supreme teacher of the Catholic faith. The Pope receives his authority from Christ as a successor of Saint Peter. All Catholics are obliged to respect and obey the Pope as the representative of Christ for the whole Church.

PREFIGUREMENT: A person, place, or thing that took place before Jesus was born, but which foretold some event in Jesus' life. For example, when God gave bread to his people while they were in the desert during the Exodus, it *prefigured* the day when Jesus would give his people the Bread of Life, the Holy Eucharist.

PRIEST: Someone who is chosen to pray and offer sacrifice to God on behalf of others. Many religions have or had priests. The sacramental priesthood was given to us by Christ, who passed it on to his apostles.

PRIESTHOOD OF THE FAITHFUL: The truth that all Christians share in the priesthood of Jesus through their Baptism. Thus we are chosen by God to pray and offer personal sacrifices to God on behalf of all mankind. We exercise our priesthood best by attending Holy Mass.

PROCREATION: One of the two purposes of marriage. Procreation means that the husband and wife cooperate with God in bringing children into the world.

PROMISED LAND: The special land, also known as Palestine or the Holy Land, which God promised to give to his people in the Old Testament.

PROPHECIES: The messages which God gave to his spokesmen (the prophets). Prophecies in the Old Testament were meant to bring people back to God and to tell them about coming events, especially the birth and life of the Messiah.

PROPHETS: Men who were chosen by God to be his spokesmen to the people. Saint John the Baptist was the last and greatest of God's prophets.

PSALMS: Prayer-poems and hymns inspired by God and found in the Old Testament. Many were written by King David of Jerusalem. The Church uses the Psalms every day in the Mass and other official prayers.

PRUDENCE: One of the four cardinal virtues. Prudence helps us to do good and avoid evil by making correct decisions in life.

REAL PRESENCE: The term which expresses our belief that Jesus is *really and truly* present with us in the Holy Eucharist. Christ's real presence may be physical or sacramental. When we pray before the Blessed Sacrament we believe that we are just as much in Christ's presence as his apostles were two thousand years ago.

RECONCILIATION: The act of re-establishing friendship between two or more persons. In Christian vocabulary reconciliation refers to the truth that Jesus, by his death and Resurrection, brought us back to friendship with God. God never stopped being our Friend, but by original sin we refused *his* friendship. Whenever we sin we are refusing friendship with God, and stand in need of reconciliation through the sacrament of Penance.

REDEEM: To free someone from slavery by buying freedom for the person. Jesus redeemed us from slavery to sin and the devil by his death and Resurrection.

REDEEMER: A title for Jesus Christ since he *redeemed* us from sin.

REPENT: To be very sorry for one's sins and to promise to give up sin in the future. John the Baptist preached *repentance* as the way of preparing for the coming of Jesus. Jesus demands that we repent and believe his good news if we want to reach heaven.

RITE (RITES): 1. A rite is a particular way of celebrating the sacraments according to the rules of the Church. For example, there is a detailed *rite* for baptizing people. 2. Rite can also mean a whole group of Christians who share a common way of worship and of living the faith. There are five different rites or kinds of Catholics in the Church. All of us profess the same faith. The two largest rites are the Roman Catholics and the Byzantine Catholics.

ROMAN CATHOLICS: Catholics whose ways of worship and of living the faith come from the customs of the city of Rome. Roman Catholics make up the largest number of members in the Church. Roman Catholics are also called Western Rite Catholics.

SACRAMENT: A visible sign or ceremony given to us by Jesus in order to give us sanctifying grace. There are seven sacraments in the Church: Baptism, Confirmation, Holy Eucharist, Penance, Anointing, Holy Orders, and Matrimony.

SACRAMENTAL: A sacramental is a sacred sign that prepares us to receive grace, especially though the sacraments.

SACRAMENTAL GRACE: The supernatural help we receive from God through the sacraments. Each sacrament gives its own kind of help. For example, Holy Orders helps a priest to preach and offer worship with a pure heart, while Matrimony helps a man and woman to love each other and be good parents.

SACRED CHRISM: A special oil blessed by a bishop and used in the sacraments of Baptism, Confirmation, and Holy Orders. It has a very beautiful scent which symbolizes the attraction of goodness and holiness. Anointing with chrism shows that we have been called by God to serve him as prophets, priests, and kings in Christ.

SACRED MYSTERIES: An ancient title for the Holy Eucharist and the Mass.

SACRIFICE: The act of offering to God something that is dear to us. As an act of worship, sacrifice means the offering of a victim to God by a priest.

SACRIFICE OF THE MASS: The greatest worship which the Church gives to God. In this Sacrifice, the priest offers God the most precious gift we have: the Body and Blood of Jesus Christ. At the end of the Eucharistic Prayer, the priest lifts up the consecrated Host and chalice to show us that he is offering Christ up to God in sacrifice.

SACRILEGE: A serious mistreatment of people, places, or things that have been consecrated to God. A *sacrilegious* Communion means that someone has received the Blessed Sacrament while being in the state of mortal sin.

SALVATION HISTORY: The events in human history that have been especially connected with the salvation of mankind. It began with the creation of man and reached its greatest point with the life of Christ. The work and preaching of the Catholic Church is a continuation of salvation history. It will be completed at the end of the world.

SANCTIFYING GRACE: The life of God in our souls by which we are made the adopted children of the Father, brothers and sisters of Jesus Christ, and temples of the Holy Spirit. We first receive sanctifying grace at Baptism, and it is increased in us with the reception of the other sacraments.

SEVEN GIFTS OF THE HOLY SPIRIT: These are seven supernatural powers we receive at Baptism and which are strengthened at Confirmation. They are wisdom, understanding, knowledge, counsel, fortitude, piety, and fear of the Lord.

SIGN: A symbol that is meant to bring a message to those who see it. A sign can be visible (such as a stop light) or verbal (words). The sacraments are seven *sacred* signs for they bring us special messages from Christ.

SIGN OF ANOINTING: The priest anoints the person with the oil of the sick, ordinarily on the person's forehead and on the palms of his hands while saying: "Through this holy anointing may the Lord in his love and mercy help you with the grace of the Holy Spirit. May the Lord who frees you from sin save you and raise you up." The message of this sign is that of spiritual healing and salvation.

SIGN OF BAPTISM: The priest (or in an emergency any person) pours water over the forehead of the person being baptized while saying: "I baptize you in the name of the Father, and of the Son, and of the Holy Spirit." The message is that of cleansing from sin and dedication to the Trinity.

SIGN OF CONFIRMATION: The bishop (or in some cases a priest) imposes his hand on the head of the person and anoints him with *chrism* while saying: "Be sealed with the gift of the Holy Spirit." The message is that of spiritual strength and power in the Holy Spirit.

SIGN OF THE HOLY EUCHARIST: The priest saying the words of consecration over the gifts of bread and wine: "This is my Body. . . . This is the cup of my Blood. . . ." The message is that of sacrifice and of spiritual nourishment.

SIGN OF HOLY ORDERS: The bishop lays hands upon the one to be ordained priest. After the imposition of hands, the bishop prays. "We ask you, all-powerful Father, give these servants of yours the dignity of the presbyterate. Renew the Spirit of holiness within them. By your divine gift may they attain the second degree of holy orders and exemplify right conduct in their lives." The message is one of spiritual power and holiness in service to the Church.

SIGN OF MATRIMONY: The man and the woman vow their lifelong love to one another. The words for this vow may vary from place to place. The message is that of lifelong unity and openness to new human lives.

SIGN OF PENANCE: The penitent who is truly sorry with a firm purpose of amendment confesses his sins to a priest, and the confessor responds with the prayer of absolution: ". . . I absolve you from your sins in the name of the Father, and of the Son, and of the Holy Spirit." The message is that of humility and forgiveness.

SIN: A deliberate offense against God's holy law in one's thoughts, words, actions, or lack of action. Sin can be either mortal or venial. *Mortal* sins destroy the life of God within us and must be privately confessed to an ordained priest. *Venial* sins can also be forgiven by other devotional acts, for example, receiving Communion or an Act of Contrition.

SOUL: The invisible or spiritual part of man. The soul gives life to the human body. It is *immortal* and will live on after death in heaven, purgatory, or hell. At the end of the world, the soul will be reunited with the body at the resurrection of the dead.

SOURCE OF ALL GRACE: A title for Jesus Christ. This reminds us that all grace (supernatural help from God) comes to us from Jesus.

SUPERNATURAL: Something that is above the powers of man or of nature. A supernatural event can be done only by God, who is the Lord and Creator of all things.

TABERNACLE: The special, solid and immovable container, often adorned with symbols of Jesus, in which the Blessed Sacrament is kept. Every Catholic church has a tabernacle in it. Thus Jesus remains within the church in a very special way. A vigil light burns night and day before the tabernacle to remind us that Christ is present.

TEMPERANCE: One of the four cardinal virtues. Temperance helps us to enjoy pleasures with moderation. It helps us to become mature, disciplined Christians.

TEMPTATION: The urge to commit sin. We are tempted in three ways: by the world (anti-Christian values in society), the flesh (our selfish desires), and the devil (Satan and his band of evil angels). Temptations are *not* sins; we can either conquer them or give in to them. Only by giving in do we commit sin.

THEOLOGICAL VIRTUES: These are the three supernatural powers of faith, hope, and charity. They are called *theological* because they deal directly with our relationship with God.

TOTAL CONSECRATION TO MARY: The act of giving ourselves and all that we have to Mary, the Mother of Jesus. We do this because Mary is our *Mother*. We want her to teach us how to become more like Jesus in every way.

TRADITION: The teachings of Christ that were preached by the apostles and handed down from century to century.

TRANSUBSTANTIATION: The word we use to describe the changing of bread and wine into the very Body and Blood of Christ.

TRINITY: The name we give to God that expresses our belief in the Father, the Son, and the Holy Spirit. Christians profess their faith in one God, who is three different Persons. This is a *mystery* that can never be fully understood by the limited human mind.

TRIPLE OFFICE: The term that reminds us of Jesus' mission as priest, prophet, and king. Through Baptism and Confirmation, we all share in this triple office of Christ.

TWELVE APOSTLES: The twelve men whom Jesus chose at the beginning of his public ministry. Judas, however, was replaced by Matthias. Their mission was to build the Church after the descent of the Holy Spirit. They were prepared for this by three years of close friendship with Jesus, who instructed them in his teachings. Their leader was Saint Peter, the first Pope. They were the first bishops of the Catholic Church.

TWELVE FRUITS OF THE HOLY SPIRIT: These are the signs of a healthy Christian life. They are: charity, joy, peace, patience, kindness, goodness, generosity, gentleness, faithfulness, modesty, self-control, and chastity.

VENIAL SIN: An offense against the holy law of God in a small matter. Venial sins weaken our relationship with God and are dangerous to our spiritual well-being.

VICTIM: A living being offered in sacrifice to God. In the Old Testament lambs, bulls and other animals were offered in sacrifice. The victim of the new and everlasting Testament is Jesus Christ. At every Holy Mass the priest offers him to the Father for the forgiveness of sins.

VIRTUE: A good habit that we learn which helps us to do good and avoid evil. Some virtues are prudence, justice, temperance, fortitude, humility, chastity, and prayer.

VOW: A free promise which we make to God, telling him that we will do something that is good and pleasing in his sight. Every Christian has made a Baptismal Vow or Baptismal Promise to God—a private vow. This vow says that we will do good, avoid evil, and live according to the teachings of Christ and his Church.

WEDDING PROMISES: The solemn promise to each other which a man and woman make on their wedding day. They promise to love one another and remain faithful to each other until death. This promise can never be revoked, not even by a civil divorce.

WILL OF GOD: The plan which God has for every human being. It is important that we do what God asks of us in this life. This will help us to reach heaven. God wills that all people obey his holy law. But there are some things that are meant for the individual only, such as what kind of life he or she is to live (priest, nun, married, etc.). We can learn God's will for us by prayer and by seeking the advice of our parents and priests.

WITNESS: Someone who can give testimony about someone else. In Christian vocabulary a witness is someone who gives testimony about Jesus to others. We witness to Jesus by good example, holy lives, or even by martyrdom.

WORDS OF CONSECRATION: The words which the priest says over the gifts of bread and wine during the Mass. By these words they are changed into the Body and Blood of Jesus Christ. These words are: "This is my Body. . . . This is the cup of my Blood. . . ."

WORSHIP: The praise, adoration, and sacrifice which we offer to God in prayer. Only God may be worshipped, for he alone is the Lord and Creator of all things. We do *not* worship Mary, the angels or the saints. We honor them because they are dear to God.

YAHWEH: The name of God which he revealed to Moses. It means "I AM." This reminds us that God is the source of all life and of every living thing.

Prayers

THE SIGN OF THE CROSS

In the name of the Father, and of the Son, and of the Holy Spirit. *Amen.*

OUR FATHER

Our Father who art in heaven, hallowed be thy name. Thy kingdom come. Thy will be done on earth, as it is in heaven. Give us this day our daily bread, and forgive us our trespasses, as we forgive those who trespass against us, and lead us not into temptation, but deliver us from evil. *Amen.*

HAIL MARY

Hail Mary, full of grace, the Lord is with thee. Blessed art thou among women, and blessed is the fruit of thy womb, Jesus.

Holy Mary, Mother of God, pray for us sinners now and at the hour of our death. *Amen.*

GLORY BE

Glory be to the Father, and to the Son, and to the Holy Spirit. As it was in the beginning, is now, and ever shall be, world without end. *Amen.*

MORNING OFFERING

O Jesus, through the Immaculate Heart of Mary I offer thee my prayers, works, joys, and sufferings of this day in union with the Holy Sacrifice of the Mass throughout the world.

I offer them for all the intentions of thy Sacred Heart: the salvation of souls, reparation for sin, the reunion of all Christians.

I offer them for the intentions of our Bishops and of all Apostles of Prayer, and in particular for those recommended by our Holy Father this month. *Amen.*

THE APOSTLES' CREED

I believe in God,
    the Father Almighty,
    creator of heaven and earth.
I believe in Jesus Christ,
    his only Son, our Lord.
He was conceived by the power of the
    Holy Spirit
    and born of the Virgin Mary.
He suffered under Pontius Pilate,
    was crucified, died, and was buried.
    He descended into hell.
On the third day he rose again.
He ascended into heaven
    and is seated at the right
    hand of the Father.
    He will come again to judge
    the living and the dead.
I believe in the Holy Spirit,
    the holy catholic Church,
    the communion of saints,
    the forgiveness of sins,
    the resurrection of the body,
    and the life everlasting.

Amen.

ACT OF FAITH

O my God, I firmly believe that thou art one God in three Divine Persons: Father, Son, and Holy Spirit. I believe that thy Divine Son became man and died for our sins, and that he will come to judge the living and the dead. I believe these and all the truths that the Holy Catholic Church teaches, because thou hast revealed them, who can neither deceive nor be deceived. *Amen.*

ACT OF HOPE

O my God, relying on thy infinite goodness and promises, I hope to obtain pardon of my sins, the help of thy grace, and life everlasting, through the merits of Jesus Christ, my Lord and Redeemer. *Amen.*

ACT OF LOVE

O my God, I love thee above all things, with my whole heart and soul, because thou art all good and worthy of all my love. I love my neighbor as myself for the love of thee. I forgive all who have injured me and ask pardon of all whom I have injured. *Amen.*

ACT OF CONTRITION

O my God, I am heartily sorry for having offended thee. I detest all my sins because of thy just punishments, but most of all because they offend thee, my God, who art all good and deserving of all my love. I firmly resolve, with the help of thy grace, to confess my sins, to do penance, and to amend my life. *Amen.*

THE ANGELUS

V. The angel of the Lord declared unto Mary.
R. And she conceived of the Holy Spirit.

Hail Mary. . . .

V. Behold the handmaid of the Lord.
R. Be it done to me according to thy word.

Hail Mary. . . .

V. And the Word was made flesh.
R. And dwelt among us.

Hail Mary. . . .
V. Pray for us, O holy Mother of God.

R. That we may be made worthy of the promises of Christ.

Let us pray. Pour forth, we beseech thee, O Lord, thy grace into our hearts, that we, to whom the Incarnation of Christ thy Son was made known by the message of an angel, may by his Passion and Cross be brought to the glory of his Resurrection. Through the same Christ Our Lord. *Amen.*

MYSTERIES OF THE ROSARY

The Joyful Mysteries

1. The Annunciation.
2. The Visitation.
3. The Nativity.
4. The Presentation.
5. The Finding in the Temple.

The Sorrowful Mysteries

1. The Agony in the Garden.
2. The Scourging at the Pillar.
3. The Crowning with Thorns.
4. The Carrying of the Cross.
5. The Crucifixion.

The Glorious Mysteries

1. The Resurrection.
2. The Ascension.
3. The Descent of the Holy Spirit.
4. The Assumption.
5. The Coronation.

The Luminous Mysteries

1. The Baptism of Christ in the Jordan.
2. The Wedding Feast of Cana.
3. The Proclamation of the Kingdom of God.
4. The Transfiguration of Our Lord.
5. The Institution of the Holy Eucharist.

LITANY OF LORETO

Lord, have mercy on us.
Christ, have mercy on us.
Lord, have mercy on us.
Christ, hear us.
Christ, graciously hear us.
God the Father of heaven,
have mercy on us.
God the Son, Redeemer of the world,
have mercy on us.
God the Holy Spirit,
have mercy on us.
Holy Trinity, One God,
have mercy on us.

Holy Mary, *pray for us.**
Holy Mother of God,
Holy Virgin of virgins,
Mother of Christ,
Mother of divine grace,
Mother most pure,
Mother most chaste,
Mother inviolate,
Mother undefiled,
Mother most amiable,
Mother most admirable,
Mother of good counsel,
Mother of the Church,
Mother of our Creator,
Mother of our Savior,
Virgin most prudent,
Virgin most venerable,
Virgin most renowned,
Virgin most powerful,
Virgin most merciful,
Virgin most faithful,
Mirror of justice,
Seat of wisdom,
Cause of our joy,
Spiritual vessel,
Vessel of honor,
Singular vessel of devotion,

Mystical rose,
Tower of David,
Tower of ivory,
House of gold,
Ark of the covenant,
Gate of Heaven,
Morning star,
Health of the sick,
Refuge of sinners,
Comforter of the afflicted,
Help of Christians,
Queen of Angels,
Queen of Patriarchs,
Queen of Prophets,
Queen of Apostles,
Queen of Martyrs,
Queen of Confessors,
Queen of Virgins,
Queen of all Saints,
Queen conceived without original sin,
Queen assumed into heaven,
Queen of the most holy Rosary,
Queen of peace,

Lamb of God, who take away the sins of the world, *spare us, O Lord.*
Lamb of God, who take away the sins of the world, *graciously hear us, O Lord.*
Lamb of God, who take away the sins of the world, *have mercy on us.*

Pray for us, O holy Mother of God.
That we may be made worthy of the promises of Christ.

Let us pray: Grant, we beseech Thee, O Lord God, unto us Thy servants, that we may rejoice in continual health of mind and body; and, by the glorious intercession of blessed Mary ever Virgin, may be delivered from present sadness, and enter into the joy of Thine eternal gladness. Through Christ our Lord. *Amen.*

THE STATIONS OF THE CROSS

1. Jesus is condemned to death.
2. Jesus carries his Cross.
3. Jesus falls the first time.
4. Jesus meets his Mother.
5. Jesus is helped by Simon of Cyrene.
6. Veronica wipes the face of Jesus.
7. Jesus falls a second time.
8. Jesus speaks to the women.
9. Jesus falls a third time.
10. Jesus is stripped of his clothes.
11. Jesus is nailed to the Cross.
12. Jesus dies on the Cross.
13. Jesus is taken down from the Cross.
14. Jesus is placed in the tomb.

PRAYER FOR THE POPE

Father of Providence, look with love on *N.* our Pope, your appointed successor to St. Peter on whom you built your Church. May he be the visible center and foundation of our unity in faith and love. Grant this through Our Lord Jesus Christ, your Son, who lives and reigns with you and the Holy Spirit, one God, for ever and ever. *Amen.*

PRAYER FOR A BISHOP

Lord our God, you have chosen your servant *N.* to be a shepherd of your flock in the tradition of the apostles. Give him a spirit of courage and right judgment, a spirit of knowledge and love. By governing with fidelity those entrusted to his care may he build your Church as a sign of salvation for the world. We ask this through Our Lord Jesus Christ, your Son, who lives and reigns with you and the Holy Spirit, one God, for ever and ever. *Amen.*

PRAYER FOR VOCATIONS
by POPE JOHN PAUL II

O Jesus, our Good Shepherd, bless all our parishes with numerous priests, deacons, men and women in religious life, consecrated laity and missionaries, according to the needs of the entire world, which you love and wish to save.

We especially entrust our community to you; grant us the spirit of the first Christians, so that we may be a cenacle of prayer, in loving acceptance of the Holy Spirit and his gifts.

Assist our pastors and all who live a consecrated life. Guide the steps of those who have responded generously to your call and are preparing to receive holy orders or to profess the evangelical counsels.

Look with love on so many well-disposed young people and call them to follow you. Help them to understand that in you alone can they attain to complete fulfillment.

To this end we call on the powerful intercession of Mary, Mother and Model of all vocations. We beseech you to sustain our faith with the certainty that the Father will grant what you have commanded us to ask. *Amen.*

PRAYER FOR UNITY OF THE CHURCH

Almighty and merciful God, you willed that the different nations should become one people through your Son. Grant in your kindness that those who glory in being known as Christians may put aside their differences and become one in truth and charity, and that all men, enlightened by the true faith, may be united in fraternal communion in the one Church. Through Christ Our Lord. *Amen.*

ANIMA CHRISTI

Soul of Christ, sanctify me.
Body of Christ, save me.
Blood of Christ, inebriate me.
Water from the side of Christ, wash me.
Passion of Christ, strengthen me.
O good Jesus, hear me;
Within thy wounds hide me;
Suffer me not to be separated from thee;
From the malignant enemy defend me;
In the hour of my death call me,
And bid me come to Thee,
That with Thy Saints I may praise Thee
for ever and ever. *Amen.*

MEMORARE

Remember, O most gracious Virgin Mary, that never was it known that anyone who fled to thy protection, implored thy help, or sought thy intercession, was left unaided. Inspired with this confidence, I fly unto thee, O Virgin of Virgins, my Mother: to thee do I come, before thee I stand, sinful and sorrowful. O Mother of the Word Incarnate, despise not my petitions, but in thy mercy hear and answer me. *Amen.*

PRAYER TO ST. MICHAEL

St. Michael, the Archangel, defend us in battle. Be our protection against the wickedness and snares of the devil. May God rebuke him, we humbly pray, and do thou, O prince of the heavenly hosts, by the power of God, thrust into hell Satan and the other evil spirits who prowl about the world seeking the ruin of souls. *Amen.*

THE PRAYER OF FATIMA

O my Jesus, forgive us our sins, save us from the fires of hell, and lead all souls into heaven, especially those in most need of thy mercy. *Amen.*

SPIRITUAL COMMUNION

My Jesus, as I cannot receive thee now in the Most Holy Blessed Sacrament, I ask thee to come into my heart, and make it like thy heart. *Amen.*

PRAYER TO MY GUARDIAN ANGEL

Angel of God, my guardian dear, To whom God's love commits me here, Ever this day be at my side, To light and guard, to rule and guide. *Amen.*

EXAMINATION OF CONSCIENCE

Come, O Holy Spirit, and help me to remember my sins. Give me the honesty I need to reflect upon my thoughts, words, and actions of this day. Amen.

FIRST COMMANDMENT: "I, the Lord, am your God. You shall not have other gods besides me."

This Commandment forbids us to worship anyone or anything besides the one true God, the Father, Son, and Holy Spirit. We worship him by Acts of Faith, Hope, and Charity; by prayer, and by self-denial.

1. Do I truly love God more than anyone or anything else?
2. Do I say my prayers every morning and night?
3. Are there "false gods" such as popularity, fashionable clothing, horoscopes or other superstitious practices, that I worship by giving them more attention than I give to the true God?

SECOND COMMANDMENT: "You shall not take the name of the Lord your God in vain."

This Commandment forbids us to misuse God's name (God, Jesus, Christ, Lord) in cursing or swearing. We must respect this Holy Name at all times and the names of his holy ones too.

1. Did I use any swear words that included God's name?
2. Did I use the name of Jesus Christ as an expression of surprise or anger?

3. Did I joke about God or religion, including Mary and the saints?

THIRD COMMANDMENT: "Remember to keep holy the Lord's Day."

This Commandment tells us to attend Holy Mass on Sundays and Holy Days of Obligation. It reminds us that any unnecessary work or shopping should be avoided on these days.

1. Have I been faithful to Sunday and Holy Day Masses (which can also be celebrated on Saturday evenings or on the night before the Holy Day)?
2. Have I prepared for Sunday Mass, especially by going to confession if I have sinned?

FOURTH COMMANDMENT: "Honor your father and mother."

This Commandment orders us to show respect and loving obedience to our parents and also to honor others in authority over us, such as teachers and government leaders (as long as they do not tell us to do things which are against God's law).

1. Have I shown love and respect for my parents, even when they punish me?
2. Do I help my parents by doing my chores and obeying their orders? Do I pray for them?
3. Do I listen to my teacher(s) and do the homework they assign?
4. Do I obey civil laws, including those which forbid the use of drugs or alcohol for minors?

FIFTH COMMANDMENT: "You shall not kill."

This Commandment forbids, not just actual murder, but even those actions that are dangerous to the life of the body and the life of the soul.

1. Do I have serious thoughts of anger and hatred toward others?
2. Do I do what I can to oppose murderous actions such as abortion, suicide, or euthanasia (the taking of the life of someone who is incurably ill or dying)?
3. Have I gotten drunk or used drugs? These things threaten human life.
4. Have I neglected the life of my soul by keeping company with those who lead me to sin?

SIXTH AND NINTH COMMANDMENTS: "You shall not commit adultery; you shall not covet your neighbor's wife."

These two Commandments deal with our human sexuality. Adultery means sexual relations between two persons one or both of whom are married, but not to each other. Here to covet means that we desire or want the spouse of another person. Although these are things that happen to adults, they carry a message for you too.

1. Do I respect the gift of sex and the human body, both my own and those of others?
2. Do I realize that sex is for married people so that they can have children and show their love for one another?
3. Do I encourage the wrong use of sexuality by myself or among my friends by looking at magazines or movies that degrade sex? Do I realize that sex is a pledge of spiritual communion between a man and a woman joined in the Sacrament of Matrimony?

4. Do I try to be chaste in my thoughts, words, and actions by myself and with others? Do I realize that sex outside of marriage and masturbation are mortal sins?
5. Do I realize that it is dangerous to my soul to spend time in impure daydreaming about sexual activities? This can easily lead me to commit sins by myself or with others.
6. Do I realize that sexual desires are good and are given to me by God so that I will one day use them properly in marriage?
7. Do I remember to pray to the Virgin Mary and Saint Joseph who are models of purity? Do I ask them to show me a healthy respect for human sexuality? To help me when I am tempted to sin against chastity?

SEVENTH AND TENTH COMMANDMENTS: "You shall not steal; you shall not covet your neighbor's goods."

These two Commandments deal with respecting the rights and property of others. They forbid us to take what does not belong to us, and to avoid even the desire to take things.

1. Have I shoplifted?
2. Have I destroyed the property of others: painted on buildings, purposely broken a window, or ripped up someone's homework?
3. Have I taken someone else's possessions: records, cassette tapes, books, magazines, clothing?
4. If I have a job, do I do it properly or do I waste time on the job? This is like stealing my boss' money since I do not really work for it.
5. Am I envious about the things my friends have and show this by my unkind words to them or to others about them?
6. Do I dislike someone simply because I am envious of his good looks, his talent in sports or school, or his popularity?

EIGHTH COMMANDMENT: "You shall not bear false witness against your neighbor."

This Commandment tells us always to be honest and truthful; it forbids us to say anything that would damage the good reputation of others.

1. Do I have the habit of lying?
2. Do I lie in order to avoid punishment or to make myself look great in the eyes of my friends? Am I afraid I will not be accepted by others unless I make myself seem better than I am?
3. Do I gossip and spread rumors about others, even if I think they are true? Do I find pleasure in telling my friends about the sins and faults of other students?
4. If a friend tells me a secret, do I keep it to myself or do I let someone else "in" on it? Do I know that telling the secrets of others is a misuse of friendship and a sin?

You do not have to use this entire examination of conscience every night. It may be more helpful to choose one Commandment each night and think about it in relation to your life.

ART CREDITS

PHOTOGRAPHS:
Gary Fuchs, pp. 70, 98, 116, 119, 120, 132
Victor Puccetti, pp. 36, 102
William Short, p. 144
UPI/Bettman, p. 14